FUNDRAISING
SECRETS

The Underground Playbook For Non Profits to Fundraise Fast, Grow Sponsors, Build A Massive Donor List, UpSurge Donations & Impact The World.

Bethany,
Let's Impact the World !
Maya McNulty
Fundraising
maverick

Maya McNulty

Best Selling Author

FUNDRAISING SECRETS

The Underground Playbook For Non Profits to Fundraise Fast, Grow Sponsors, Build A Massive Donor List, UpSurge Donations & Impact The World.

Published in Schenectady, New York by Orchard Publishing Media.

https://upthebiz.com/
https://mayamcnulty.com/
https://www.facebook.com/fundraisingsecrets/
https://www.linkedin.com/in/mayamcnulty/
https://www.instagram.com/mayamcnultyinspires/
https://twitter.com/mayamcnulty
www.fundraisefast.com
www.fundraisingsecrets.org
www.fundpreneur.org
www.fundraisingsecret.com
www.mcnultylinks.com

Cover Design: German Creative
Photography: Chris Milian

Orchard Publishing Media
Schenectady, NY 12309
USA
ISBN # paperback 978-0-9600411-2-1
ISBN # eBook 978-0-9600411-3-8

Printed in the United States of America

"We ourselves feel that what we are doing is just a drop in the ocean. But the ocean would be less because of that missing drop."

Mother Teresa

FUNDPRENEUR
MANIFESTO

A FUNDPRENEUR
is a **HEART CENTERED LEADER.**

FUNDPRENEURS
take no **B.S.** and **MAKE NO APOLOGIES
FOR SERVING THE PUBLIC.**

FUNDPRENEURS
UNITE and **THRIVE** knowing that
together we will prevail.

FUNDPRENEURS
will **FIGHT FOR THE CAUSE,
RAISE AWARENESS AND SERVE
WITH HUMILITY.**

FUNDPRENEURS
are **RESOURCEFUL, COMPASSIONATE**
and **"PHILANTHROPY"** is our
middle name.

FUNDPRENEURS
deploy the organization's task **WITH
HONOR** and **CHAMPIONS THE MISSION.**

FUNDPRENEURS
ENRICHES LIVES and **PUTS
ETHICS BEFORE CONVERSIONS.**

FUNDPRENEURS

DEFINE STRENGTH IN NUMBERS.
BELIEVE IN THE CAUSE.
CREATE THE FUTURE.
BUILD FUNDRAISING EMPIRES.
IMPACT THE WORLD.

FUNDPRENEURS

DRIVEN AND INSPIRED
KNOWING THAT WE ARE
MAKING FUNDRAISING FUN.

I AM A FUNDPRENEUR.

Fundraising Secrets

Mini Manifesto for Fundraising Secrets

I AM A FUND-PRENEUR

I DEFINE STRENGTH IN NUMBERS

I BELIEVE IN THE CAUSE

I CREATE THE FUTURE

I BUILD FUNDRAISNG EMPIRES

I IMPACT THE WORLD

I MAKE FUNDRAISING FUN

Dedication

To my Mom and Dad, thank you for your wisdom and unconditional love. You encouraged me to always be true to myself and serve with humility.

To my husband Ron and daughter Alana, who have given me reason to try to make this world a better place. You are my motivation, inspiration and loves in my life.

Contents

Acknowledgments

I would like to extend my sincere gratitude to Wilma Schmeler, who wholehearted gave me inspiration to write this book and solve the problem of fundraising for non profits. A few years back, she had a conversation with me about the slickest fundraising event she had ever attended in her lifetime. It was an event I had created to benefit the Capital District Special Olympics, NY. That conversation carried on and led to another successful event. Wilma felt my energy and asked to be on the Steering Committee. She often reminded me of spotting a leader and what's possible when someone's truly passionate about the nonprofits mission. That one conversation took me on this journey and has resulted in *Fundraising Secrets*. You will see many things I learned from Wilma throughout these pages. Without her support and ideas, this book wouldn't have been possible. Wilma is a dear friend and fellow Philanthropist. I'm grateful to have been mentored by this charismatic woman.

I want to thank Shari Quinn for teaching me the fundamentals of writing not just a book but a movement. I want to thank Neal Johnson, former President of Special Olympics NY, for recognizing that spark in my eyes, and passion for volunteering, plus believing in my vision. I want to thank the production team at SACC Studios and Randall Hogue for giving me a platform to share my message. I want to thank my brilliant friend Katie DeSarbo for her wisdom and mentorship. I want to thank Darcy Knapp, of SEO Web Mechanics, for supporting numerous fundraisers, creating the websites and driving traffic. I want to thank Paul DeBiase, manager at Union College, for his endless support and contributions. I want to thank Melissa O'Reilly for her trust and partnership with several fundraising projects. I want to thank the National Alliance on Mental Health NYS, for giving me an opportunity to teach Fundraising Secrets to their staff. I want to thank my parents for their love and encouragement. I want to thank my husband Ron and daughter Alana for being my support team, my inspiration and motivation.

What Is Fundraising Secrets?

Fundraising Secrets is not just another "how to fundraise" book that was written by someone who has never fund raised.

It is NOT a book that contains ideas, scripts and strategies that sound good on paper but have never been tested.

Fundraising Secrets reveals ninja tricks by leveraging best practices, systems and strategies to make your nonprofit go from struggling to impactful in just a few short months. Throughout each chapter you will discover an easy to follow, step by step blueprint that teaches you how to fundraise fast, grow sponsorship relationships, effortlessly build a massive list of donors, and impact the world.

Fundraising Secrets will help your organization find its voice and increase company moral while impacting the world.

Fundraising Secrets will empower you to attract and build a community of raving fans. Engage philanthropists and volunteer leaders in a results oriented way encouraging BIG corporations to write significant checks to your cause.

Fundraising Secrets will attract new opportunities seamlessly and effortlessly month after month while strengthening your brand awareness and achieving your organization's mission.

Fundraising Secrets will empower your organization and impact the world.

Your organization matters and this book is the blueprint to guide you.

"Volunteers do not necessarily have the time;
they have the heart."

— Elizabeth Andrew

Introductions

Congratulations on purchasing this book! You now have in your hands the only guide that you will ever need to achieve extraordinary success in fundraising.

This book will be the only resource you will ever need to master the art of fundraising and create a legacy for the organization that you build and serve. Just follow the step by step blue print and the result will be a successful fundraising campaign.

When I was 15 years old, my Art teacher Mrs. Bartier, introduced me to volunteering at the City Mission during Thanksgiving, feeding the hungry. It was a different kind of volunteering than I was accustomed to at Temple. As a young kid, on Sundays, my family would volunteer at The Hindu Temple in Schenectady, NY. My mom cooked for hours in the kitchen with the other Indian ladies. My dad sang in the Hindu choir. We would be at Temple for 3-4 hours every Sunday. I'm Guyanese, Indian, I was born in South America, Guyana. My parents and I came to America in 1979. I can remember being so fascinated with the American culture and often rebelled against my parent's wishes. I would often run off to see what my American friends were doing. I got into loads of trouble with my parents because they didn't understand volunteering in American culture. They had this belief that the only place you volunteered was at church. To summarize the story, this is when I learned how to volunteer in American culture and what an impact it would later portray in my work, community and life.

I always enjoy volunteering. What I liked most is the fun I have! It is a bonus to meet people from all walks of life and build relationships. I love the mission of serving with humility. My parents didn't understand this volunteering stuff. My mom thought I used volunteering as an excuse for not helping her clean the house and make Thanksgiving dinner. Maybe subconsciously I did, but I've always set a beautiful Thanksgiving table. Frankly, I never liked all the cooking and cleaning up after Thanksgiving dinner. Although, Thanksgiving is one of my happiest family memories, I can best remember the joy I feel serving others.

Junior year of high school was the first time I was quoted in the local newspaper for my volunteer contributions.

The Schenectady Gazette (The Daily Gazette)
November 24, 1989

Testimonials

I had the pleasure of professionally knowing Maya McNulty for the past several years, and nominating her in 2017 for the distinguished award given by the Schenectady County Human Rights Commission for her commitment to excellence, entrepreneurship and philanthropy. Her continuous dedication has helped enhance small business development, women entrepreneurs and the local economy. She is passionate about sharing best practices to help other professional and aspiring business owners maximize success. She is a first-class winner with a magnetic energy of positivity, creativity and integrity. If you are interested in business development coaching, want to learn more about how to increase your revenue margins or simply increase your networking opportunities, Maya is indeed the professional to talk to. I wholeheartedly recommend her without any reservation.

Shari W. Quinn: Author | Educator | Speaker | University of California Berkeley

Maya is a dynamic individual, always putting all her energy into every project. She is dependable and enjoyable to work with. I highly recommend Maya if you need help with your business, a project or a fundraising event! She is amazing.

Darcy Knapp, MBA: President SEO Web Mechanics

Maya is a tremendous innovator and business leader. She is dedicated, creative, and inspiring. Her personality is people centered and she is a wonderful communicator. Maya is dedicated to helping others through her business, TV show, and through her not for profit work. She is an amazing person filled with a passion for life and compassion for others.

Sharon Burstein: Transforming Global Motivational and Leadership Speaker – Award Winning Author | International Consultant and PR Strategist

Case Studies

Since 2016, I have been working with different nonprofits using the techniques I developed in *Fundraising Secrets*. The partnerships formed helps to raise money for initiatives such as new programs, facilities, research and scholarships.

Case Study #1

Date: March 4, 2016 - May 13, 2016

Non Profit Organization: Leukemia Lymphoma Society

Upstate NY/ Vermont Chapter

The Leukemia & Lymphoma Society is the world's largest voluntary health organization dedicated to funding blood cancer research, education and patient services. They offer a wide variety of programs and services in support of their mission to cure leukemia, lymphoma, Hodgkin's disease and myeloma. To improve the quality of life of patients and their families is a priority.

Event: LLS Man and Woman of the Year

Campaign Website: www.MWOY.org/uny/

Raised: $612,677 (10 Weeks Campaign)

16 Community Leaders raised over $612K in 10 weeks.

CASE STUDY #2

Date: January 1, 2017- May 18, 2017

Non Profit Organization: Special Olympics, NY

Special Olympics NY is a private nonprofit 501(c)(3) organization and is funded primarily by donations from individuals, corporations and foundations.

Event: Runway For The Gold Fashion Show

Campaign Website: www.runwayforthegold.org

Corporate Website: www.specialolympicsny.org

Raised: $36,366 (6 Weeks Campaign)

Letter from the President & CEO

Dear Friends,

I am pleased to present "Runway for the Gold", a fashion show and benefit for Special Olympics New York's State Summer Games. We are proud that our highest level of competition, State Summer Games, will be held in the Capital District Region hosted by Siena College this June 16-18, 2017.

First of all, thank you to the leaders, volunteers and local businesses. A special thanks goes to the chair of tonight's show, Maya McNulty, and her Steering Committee team and to our sponsors, Wilma and Frank Schmeler, along with our SONY staff, our wonderful models and of course all of you for being with us tonight.

However, what makes tonight even more important and special are the athletes. Runway for the Gold spotlights the talented athletes front and center stage - which is exactly where they should be. I am so proud of our community and each and every one of you here tonight for embracing our different abilities, coming together to build confidence and pride in each and every one of us, while having fun and raising funds for the athletes of Special Olympics New York. Let the show begin!

Sincerely,

Neal J. Johnson
President & CEO
Special Olympics New York

3

Our first annual "Runway for the Gold" fashion show, which was held on May 18, 2017 was a huge success! With the generous support of the models, athletes, volunteers, attendees and generous donors, we raised more than $31,000 for State Summer Games. We would like to give a special thanks to the following businesses for their support of $2,500 or more to "Runway for the Gold". Photo by Chris Milian. *Pictured left to right: McNulty and Bryce Reynolds*

CASE STUDY #3

Date: January 1, 2018 - April 12, 2018

Non Profit Organization: Special Olympics, NY

Special Olympics NY is a private nonprofit 501(c)(3) organization and is funded primarily by donations from individuals, corporations and foundations

Event: Runway For The Gold Fashion Show

Website: runwayforthegold.org

Raised: $43,141 (10 Weeks Campaign)

Photo Credit: Chris Milian / Aerial Photographer

OFF THE MASK

ENDING STIGMA: A CELEBRATION OF MENTAL WELLNESS

CASE STUDY #4

Date: January 1, 2019 – May 10, 2019

Non Profit Organization: NAMI – NYS: The National Alliance on Mental Illness

The largest, 501 (c)(3), grassroots organization dedicated to improving the lives of people living with mental illness. For over 35 years, NAMI- NYS has effectively provided and connected families, individuals, schools, and families of veterans with resources, support, free education, and advocacy to maintain vibrant and mentally healthy communities across New York State.

Event: Off The Mask – Fashion Show and Art Exhibit

Campaign Website: www.offthemask.org

Corporate Website: www.naminys.org

Raised: $100,000 (12 Weeks Campaign)

Testimonial:

"We are thrilled to report that **NAMI-NYS's** Off the Mask event was a tremendous success. Not only was it a magical and inspiring evening but it was also the most successful fundraiser ever produced by **NAMI-NYS**."

Matthew Shapiro – Associate Director Public Affairs **NAMI-NYS**

Chapter One:

Creating Your Dream Team

Secret 1: Organizing Your Dream Team

When hosting any successful fundraising event you must create your dream team. This dream team should consist of a variety of talent. That includes your community, board members, donors, and volunteers. Pay very close attention to the mix of talent you invite to contribute in your fundraising event. The strategic reason you want to do this is because each will bring a diverse network and circle of influences.

The recommended event panel line up when creating a team is:

- One Board Member
- One Staff
- Two Community Volunteers
- One Donor

Good planning starts with a five member dream team. This core group of leaders will be called The Steering Committee.

Start by recruiting a board member from the organization. Including a board member solidifies the mission of the organization. They usually are resourceful and have a proven track record of being responsible for the agency. They also feel obligated to the people they serve.

Second, recruit at least one person from the organization to help with reports, meeting minutes, communication, public relations, marketing, emails, etc. (You might be the only one in the organization, in which case, you are all in.) It's important to have an organization team member reporting back to their boss or president of the organization. This person will also manage the budget and handle any account payables. The representative from the organization will have clearly defined roles per their job requirements in addition to taking on fundraising. It's essential to lay out a written time line, job roles and responsibilities in advance. Most importantly, having a staff member on the team insures the nonprofit's logos, brand, money and concerns are running efficiently and they can tell the organization's story.

Next invite at least two community leaders to serve on your steering committee. Non Profits thrive best in communities with volunteer involvement. Seek out community leaders that are resourceful and their brand and company vision aligns with the non profits mission.

Finally, probably the most important step is to invite a past donor as a voice and member of the Steering Committee. Here's why. Past donors have empathy for the people and the organization. That's why they donated in the past. They want what's best for the organization. These donors believe in the cause and will rally to the end for the best outcome. They will use every resource they've ever collected and share systems and procedures that have worked while avoiding ones that have failed. Listening to your donors is a key strategy that will help to shorten the learning curve and position you to reaching your fundraising goals faster.

This example of a value ladder will help you visualize how volunteers can ascend to new opportunities within your organization. The value ladder gives both the organization and its volunteer's new opportunities for contribution. Once you win a volunteer take care of them. They will become more vested as they continue to ascend effortlessly and with enthusiasm.

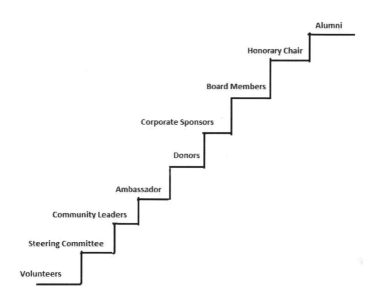

Secret #2 Respect Your Committee

Now that you've established the Steering Committee, treat them like gold. Open communication and show your organization that you will give them the support, help, tools and resources needed to run a successful campaign. Build a relationship with your Steering Committee members by consistently reaching out and asking questions. Don't undermine the Steering Committee. They are a group of volunteers collaborating for your organization's interest.

Show appreciation to the Steering Committee by hosting a Meet and Greet reception, lunch or dinner. Sending a thank you note or package in the mail consistently throughout the 12-15 weeks fundraising campaign reflects your appreciation.

Get to know your Steering Committee by creating opportunities to grow together. This will build trust and respect for the organization. Each member brings their special talent. Making them feel important reinforces their contribution, and helps to strengthen the nonprofit's mission.

Secret #3 Feasibility Study

A Feasibility study is often handled by a third party representative, usually a fundraising consultant. They interview important stakeholders in your organization and community. In short, a feasibility study is a tool that helps predict how successful your fundraising efforts will be.

In this book, *Fundraising Secrets*, I teach you the techniques I've developed empowering nonprofits to fundraise $70K -$700K in less than 12 weeks without doing a feasibility study.

Secret #4 Create a Waiting List of Dream Teamers

Once you have established your dream team and things begin to move fast, you will be getting noticed for your extraordinary talent and work. You will attract a tribe of community minded leaders, a surplus of community minded people excited about being a part your fundraising event. This is a great problem to have. One of the most creative things I've done while fundraising is compiling a waiting list. I'd recommend doing it! A waiting list provides a ready made group of qualified people to take part in your annual event. It also gives you leverage and options to work alongside some of the best, brightest and most talented professionals.

Once you've recognized your dream team and community leaders, incentivize them with tokens of appreciation. As an organization you love to receive charitable gifts of money. Volunteers like to receive certificates of appreciation and a collection of swag from the organization they serve. They will display prominently in their offices or wear as a cape of honor. Volunteers thrive when they are being thanked and feel appreciated. Incentivizing is essential to creating a winning Cult-ure. Thank every volunteer who contributed in any capacity. Treat everyone with the same respect and make sure no effort goes unnoticed.

Secret Tip #1 Recognize and pay attention to your volunteers.

Chapter Two:

Creating Drama Free Timeline and Crushing Deadlines

Secret #5 Prepare Timeline

It is essential to map out one master timeline 12 -15 weeks in advance. Your timeline should include milestones that the committee agrees on and must hit over a period of time to ensure that they are on track to meeting fundraising goals and deadlines.

It is recommended that your timeline include a detail description of goals with date and time to be stamped as completed. The fundraising process moves extremely fast. Failing to plan will construct inadequacies and cause unnecessary distractions. Avoid this at all cost. Create a drama free timeline at your first Steering Committee meeting. Then follow up at weekly scheduled Steering Committee meetings to ensure everyone is participating and on schedule.

When constructing the timeline each Steering Committee member's job and responsibilities are outlined so that there is no loss of time or missed communication. Each role is defined in advance. This will help to insure that reaching milestone goals is attainable. Having structure to the planning and organization in advance solidifies each members responsibilities and communication is open and clear. Appointing a chair person and securing Honorary Chair people, as needed, at this time is important. This person will be the community leader for outreach and any media. The Steering Committee may cast a vote for chair person or /and co – chair persons to avoid any self – appointment if necessary.

Some important steps to follow during week one of setting up your fundraising timeline includes, planning a budget for your special event. A budget should be practical and not embarrassing / insulting to the Steering Committee. For example, if the organization wants to create a higher end event for a 100 people on a $10K budget it's doable but very stressful for the Steering Committee to fulfill such a tall order on a small budget. The Steering Committee is conscious and also understands that's why they are fundraising. So it's very important to be creative and land some in kind services. The budget should be based on the region that the special event is being held. Seasonal products might not be available for a particular type of event. Higher end events hosting 100 people at $10K dollar budget in New York City, Miami, or California is not practical based of the cost of living and other factors such as food cost. However, a $10K budget for 100 people in Upstate New York or other rural areas is possible because the food and operating cost is less.

Now that you agreed on the budget, created a timeline, defined roles, and set goals for each Steering Committee member, it's time to get to work.

Start by providing each Steering Committee member with a binder to keep track of all important documents and notes for your special event. This is extremely helpful as the week's progress and deadlines come closer. The binder process helps to stay organized and in the flow. This systematized process allows for easy access to all important documents and saves a ton of time when looking for relevant paperwork to create reports for the organization's board members and /or the president.

> Secret Tip #2: Creating a timeline in advance eliminates confusion and disconnect. This should be created during week one after the initial meet and greet of Steering Committee, Board Members, and Staff. This process will also map out important dates and deadlines.

Time Line Example:

Timeline

OFF THE MASK NAMI ART AND FASHION SHOW – MAY 10, 2019

IMPORTANT DATES:

October 30 – Committee Meeting

November 8, 30 – Committee Meeting / Board Meetings

December 4 – Begin model recruitment

December 4 - Tour Venue Hearst Media, Save the dates post cards design & Logo, Create Sponsorship packages, Create Model incentive gift boxes and letters

December 9- Committee Meeting

January 7 - Send Out Save The Dates, Mail Sponsorship Letters, Press Release

January 30 – Committee Meeting

January 31- Models Bio's and Web links tested and active

February 15 – Meet & Greet the models Show Q & A Glenn Peter – Central Ave, Albany. 5:30pm-7:30pm Glenn Peter will provide food and donations from Bar

March 4, – Deadline for Sponsorship Inclusion in invitation

March 15 – Invitations to printer

March 22- Artist Bio's for Program Booklet deadline

March 26- Deadline for Sponsorship inclusion in Program Booklet

April 1- Mask Deadline

April 1 – Mail Invitations

April 8 – Program Booklet Edits/Print

April 8 – Models Fittings

April 15- Deadline: Collect Art, Sculptures, and Pieces for Auction; Bring to Nami Office

May 1 – RSVP Due- Fashion Show

May 10 – Show Time

June 12- ReCap Party

November: Steering Committee

- Board Meeting – November 30
- Review Budget, Fundraising Goals
- Determine Venue
- Recruit Models
- Secure domain www.offthemask.com
- Create Logo – OFF THE MASK

December: Finalize Sponsorship Packages

- Develop mailing list for Sponsor prospects, formal invitations, & Save the Dates post cards
- Continue Recruit Models- Create Fundraising Pages for All models, & Artist, etc
- Send Welcome Gift and Acknowledgement letter
- Plan Meet and Greet
- Develop Sponsorship Letter and Package
- Finalize Save the Date Post Card – Send to print
- Create Program Booklet AD offers

January: Action Steps #1

- Mail Save the Dates
- Mail Sponsorship Letters
- Send Out Press Release
- UpLoad Bio's and Build Personal Fundraising Pages for all models & artist
- Secure Emcee
- Secure Celebrity Speaker
- Secure Local Political Officials
- Secure additional committee members if needed
- Secure Live Auctioneer if needed
- Secure Event Lead Sponsor
- Follow up on all sponsors with phone calls
- Prepare Letter or Sponsorship letter for Honorary Co- Chairs or Honorary Committee (if needed)

February: Action Steps #2

- Follow up on Sponsorship with email/phone calls
- Recruit Models – Get Bio's, photos and create weblink
- Recruit Artist- Get Bio's, photos and create weblink
- Host Meet and Greet Q & A at Glenn Peter 2/15 5pm.

March: Action Steps #3

- Deadline for Sponsorship Inclusion in invitation
- Invitations to printer
- Artist Bio's for Program Booklet deadline
- Deadline for Sponsorship inclusion in Program Booklet
- Create Silent Auction for Art Work Bid Forms
- Create Candle Of Hope Table Signage (Battery Operated)
- Order Prizes for Top 3 Fundraiser
- All Fundraising kicks off March 4- May 10.(keeps the game fair for all models)

April: Action Steps #4

- Mail Invitations
- Program Booklet Edits
- Program Booklet Print
- Models Fittings
- Collect All Art for Auction
- Follow Up with the entire show production team

Models, Artist, Media, Press, Advertising, Radio, DJ, Venue, Photographers, Flowers, Vendors, Gift Bags/ Swags, Everyone etc. Follow up.

May: <u>Final Push/ Show Time!</u>

- Final Model Fittings (if needed)
- RSVP due
- Organize VIP Seating for Sponsors
- VIP Seating for Guest
- Create Swag Bags for VIP tickets (optional)

June: <u>ReCap Party</u>

The ReCap Party is for all who participated in the production of the show. That includes the Steering Committee, DJ, Artist, Models, Hair Stylist, Board Members, Video, Photographers, EVERYONE. Presentations will include Certificates of Appreciations, Thank You gifts and also serve as the official close. The final fundraising total is shared that night because donations would randomly continue to flood in after the event. It's essential to personally thank each volunteer during the recap party. It's also recommended that the Sponsors be thanked and recognized. The Recap Party will host approximately 40 people in attendance. Many restaurants will usually donate or charge you their cost.

Example of ReCap Party Script:

Recap Party Script:

Welcome Everyone!

Start with Crowd Engagement #1

- Look Right – Say, You're Awesome!!!
- Look Left –You Look Good!!!

Introduce Yourself and Team

- I'm John Smith – Member of the Steering Committee for

  _____

- Thank you to members of the Steering Committee: _____, _____, And _____ (Ask for a Massive Round of Applause)
- Thank you to _____ Event Sponsors - (Read Sponsors)
- Thank you to the Production Team – Tell A Short Story
- Tell Your Relationship Story – Thank the Venue - JP and Staff at Katie's- Thank you for your support during LLS, SONY, etc campaign,

You Serve with Humility and that's what makes You Great!

- Thank Your Family _____, _____, _____. (Tell a short Story)

What to Expect Tonight

FOOD and FUN – Slide show, Video etc.

Ask A Question. Crowd Engagement #2.

- Does This Sound Good?

Reminders

- Grab Your Certificates of Appreciation. (Tell a short story)

- We are extremely Grateful for your dedication, Love and Support. This Token Might Be Small – But, Priceless. – (Tell a story)

Crowd Engagement #3

Tell A Story – Add Value: Or Quote someone.

Les Brown – He's a motivational speaker, author, and podcaster.

 I love his work and think that he's

Every Shade of Awesomeness!

I want to Echo the words of Les Brown.

"You have that Special Gift

You Were Born For Greatness! AND

You Have Greatness Inside of YOU!"

Impact Statement

- Recap Fundraising Totals – 2017 Raised $36,366
- 2018 Raised $43,141. Profit $64,386 Year to date. Impact 129 Athletes

Summary and Closing Remarks

- Recap Thanks You. Tell short story.

Crowd Engagement #4   Ask for Permission

- Will you Join Me in re- sighting the Special Olympics Oath?

Let Me Win. But, If I Can Not Win. Let Me Brave In The ATTEMPT!

Go Win The GOLD!!! Good Luck at State Games!

Say Thank you again.

Action Step:

Introduce the next speaker

- Now, A few Words from The President or The Interim CEO, of _____.

Secret #6 Create a One Sheet Cadency Report

What is a Cadency Report?

A Cadency Report is a snap shot or an at a glance overview of all the key players, their contact information and logistics for a specific event. This report is effective because it helps to alleviate stress when it comes to managing a large group of people and their job duties.

Important things you will find on a Cadency Report:

- ✓ Event Title
- ✓ Date, Location and Time
- ✓ Venue Event Manager Contact
- ✓ Guest Capacity
- ✓ Event Ticket Price
- ✓ Committee and Volunteers Rolls
- ✓ Event Producer Contacts
- ✓ Emails and Phone Numbers
- ✓ Budget
- ✓ Meet and Greet Dates, Time and Location
- ✓ ReCap Party Dates, Time and Location
- ✓ Checklist

Example of a Fashion Show Event Cadency Report:

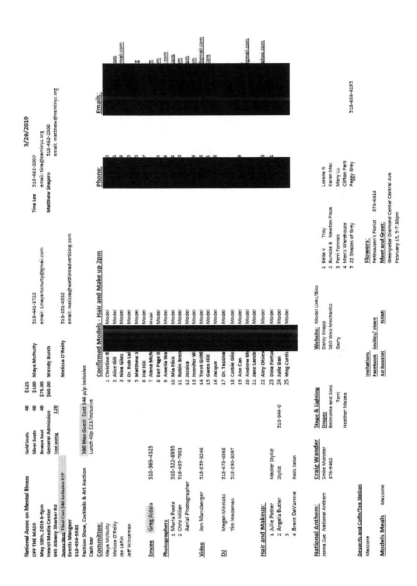

National Assoc on Mental Illness
OFF THE MASK
May 10th, 2019 6-9pm
Hearst Media Center
645 Albany Shaker Rd
~~Tickets Here: First Cost $46 inclusive P/P~~
Events Manager
518-454-5583
Fashion Show, Cocktails & Art Auction
Cash bar

Gold Seats	40	$125
Silver Seats	40	$100
Bronze Seat	40	$75.00
General Admission		$60.00
~~total seating~~	120	

300 Max Guest: Cost $46 p/p inclusive
Lunch 4tp $121 inclusive

Maya McNulty
Wendy Burch
Melissa O'Reilly

Tina Lee 518-461-2000
email: tina@namiinys.org
Matthew Shapiro 518-462-2000
email: matthew@namiinys.org 3/26/2019

Committee:
Maya McNulty
Melissa O'Reilly
Jen Laffin
Jeff Winterman

518-441-3722
email: tmayemcnulty@gmail.com

518-281-4832
email: melissa@wethinkadvertising.com

Emcee Greg Aidala 518-265-4325

Photographers
1 Maria Poole 518-312-6935
2 Chris Millan 518-442-7983
   Aerial Photographer

Video Jon Mansberger 518-639-3246

DJ
Megan Minnicks 518-478-4868
Tim Wederman 518-290-3057

Hair and Makeup:
1. Julie Porter Master Stylist
2. Angela Butler Stylist
3.
4. Brent DeVarone Rossi Salon

National Anthem:
Jenna Sue National Anthem Smile Monster 376-9462

Desserts and Coffee/Tea Station
Mezzanine

Models Meals Mezzanine

Confirmed Models – Hair and Make up 2pm
1. Christine R Model
2. Alice Gill Model
3. Nina Giles Model
4. Dr. Rob Lai Model
5. Matthew S Model
6. Hal Hill Model
7. Alana McN Model
8. Earl Page B Model
9. Amelia Wes Model
10. Mia Flick Model
11. Robin Brent Model
12. Jessica Model
13. Jennifer W Model
14. Trent Griffi Model
15. Green Hill Model
16. Jacque Model
17. Dr. Tassaina Model
18. Colbie Gilio Model
19. Ann Con Model
20. Andrew M Model
21. Janet Lamb Model
22. Aley Obsrev Model
23. Dina Fortun Model
24. Julie Ban Model
25. Meg Curtis Model

Stage & Lighting
Drapes
Belmonte and Sons Terri
Heather Mazee 518-944-0

Craig Wander

Website: Model Links/Bios
Darcy Knapp SEO Web Mechanics
Garry

Invitations
Facebook invited/ share
Ad Booklet NAMI

Flowers:
1 Bella V Troy Lorena N
2 Bumble 5 Newton Plaza Karen Mac
3 Fern Formals Mary Lu
4 Men's Warehouse Clifton Park
5 22 Shades of Grey Peggy Grey

Fethouam's Florist 374-4414
Meet and Greet:
Gleanpeter Diamond Center Central Ave
February 15, 5-7:30pm

Emails:

Phone:

518-616-4155

Secrets #7 Draft a Calling Script for Corporate Sponsor Prospects

When calling potential sponsors or donors it is best to be consistent with the dialog and message. This is accomplished by drafting a phone script. Having an In Bound and Out Bound phone script is the most efficient way to acquire donations and provide a comfortable message for your callers whether they serve as volunteers or staff.

Example of Corporate Calling Script:

Calling Script - 'Runway for the Gold' Corporate Sponsor Prospects

Hello _____,

This is _____, a student intern at Special Olympics New York, calling. I am reaching out to you to follow up on the letter you recently received inviting you to sponsor Special Olympics New York's 2nd Annual Runway for the Gold Fashion Show and Cocktail Party which will be held on Thursday, April 12th at 6 o'clock at the Mohawk River Country Club in Rexford, New York.

Our Special Olympic athletes will proudly catwalk down the Runway with community leaders showing us what they have accomplished. It promises to be an enjoyable evening of camaraderie in support of our Special Olympic athletes who are competing in this year's 49th Special Olympics New York Summer Games at Siena College in June.

Please support our athletes by sponsoring the 'Runway for the Gold'. Your support will ensure that all of our athletes have the opportunity to compete in one of the most important competitions of their lifetime at no cost to them, their families or caregivers.

Sponsorship levels, benefits and timelines are described in the information you received a few weeks ago. If you need additional information we can email it to you or please contact Sue Smith at (517) 399-1234 Ext. 123 or SSmith@nyso.org Registration and Sponsorship is also available online: runwayforthegold.org

Please note that registration for Sponsorships is due February 9th so that we can meet our printing deadline.

Thank you for considering this request, and we hope we can count on you to support and champion our Special Olympic athletes as they compete in the upcoming Special Olympics New York Summer Games at Siena College.

Again, it's _____ calling on behalf of our Special Olympics New York athletes.

THANK YOU!

_____

_____

_____

Please note:

- This is a "suggested" calling script. Use it, modify it, or just use your own words. The important thing to say up front is that you are a volunteer for Special Olympics New York.... This usually quickly relaxes people and makes them open to the reason for your call.
- For additional information that you may want to mention, please refer to the 'Letter of Invitation' and 'Brochure' that all sponsorship prospects have received.

Secret #8 Secure Venue

This is the exciting part! By now you have formed your Steering Committee and established a budget. It's time to secure the venue. There are many important considerations when securing a venue. These may vary depending on type of event but common to many are:

- Floor plan
- Venue capacity
- Up lighting
- Stage AV systems
- Microphones
- Podiums
- Number of table and chairs

- Linen
- Food Service or Caterer
- Bathrooms
- Parking Lot and Handicap Access

Utilizing a note book to document your considerations is important during then venue walk through. When meeting with the Events Manager you'll be prepared. You'll also want to get answers about in kind donations, in house grants or scholarships. Don't forget to ask about premium advertising trade, food and beverage trade, and sponsorship availabilities. You will be surprised at the generosity of each venue. You just have to ask. Remember that you are already at a NO without the Ask. So Ask! You will also need to provide your nonprofit 501c3 form and certificate of insurance. If you agree on the venue, secure it with date and time of your event. Provide a deposit to lock in the date and time so it doesn't get taken by someone else. I can't stress this enough. I've seen this happen several times. The Steering Committee and decision maker need pre approval from the board members to secure venue at the end of the walk through to avoid this situation. Once the event proposal is signed and venue secured, this will give the committee piece of mind. The momentum will start to build and everyone will be excited about the upcoming event.

Secret #9 Purchase the domain of the event.

There are several domain hosting companies on the market. The one I trust and use is GoDaddy.com I'd recommend searching for a domain name on Go Daddy that is short and easy to spell and share. I would also recommend that you purchase the .com and .org of the event name. This will prevent any other person from purchasing and owning your event name in the future.

Secret #10 Create Killer Logo and Graphics

Your brand is what people say about you when you're not in the room. It is crucial that your graphic designer create something magical that will convey your mission. An event logo is different than your corporate logo. You'll want to use your corporate logo along with the event logo to brand the event and get people excited. Your corporate logo is the master logo. Sometimes the logo is owned by the State you do business in for example New York State which has many divisions. Often times, not all divisions or jurisdictions are going to participate in your event. Therefore, the corporate logo is branded amongst all the chapters or headquarters and the event logo is specifically local to that event. If you're an independent nonprofit, not owned by the state you do work in, you probably already have your own corporate logo. That's good news. It's always a good idea to have a logo for separate events. Also, as you begin to host more and more events, you'll use a different logo to attract the ideal audience for that specific event. This will help to avoid confusion.

So where can I purchase a high quality logo? Websites such as, Fiverr.com, UpWork, and Canva have a host of graphic designers at affordable rates. You can hire several different creators at once to help move your project forward faster. You may also opt to outsource and hire a local marketing agency. I'd recommend hiring an expert graphic designer to design a high quality event logo and vector. This logo will be timeless and used across the event website, invitations, swags, media and print. The logo also becomes part of your organization's brand asset.

If your organization decides to host an annual event, the logo becomes very valuable for event invitations and media. I've witnessed organizations change their logo or branding colors midway thru the current event causing mass confusion for the audience. Don't do that. Stick with one logo and branding throughout the same event. In today's digital world sending out electronic invitations will be to your best advantage. I'd also suggest that you order double the seating physical hard copy invitations for your event. For example, if there's a 100 seat, order 200 invitations. Prepare a list of invitees 10 weeks before the special event and mail invitations 6 weeks before the event. Follow up with phone calls to VIPs and Sponsors to secure number of reserved seats and open seating available. Update your event system and paperwork to avoid overselling VIP seating. A ninja trick is to send invitations to more than one department in a particular company your organization is trying to attract. Going in from different angles and departments might attract a new ideal donor.

Secret Tip #3 Hire a graphic designer to create killer event logo.

Secret #11 Compile Donor List

I've personally worked with several nonprofits who didn't have a list or worked from an old list. Here are three solutions when working from a failing list. If your donor list is small, sponsorship list is weak, and your list is old, here's how to fix it and get more sponsors chomping at the bit to write significant checks.

#1. If your donor list is small, hack other look a-like organization's sponsors. Respectfully, attend their events and use their event booklet as a resource for leads.

Read your local newspaper, business trade magazines and online advertisements. Make the connection of what types of businesses are continually making contributions to causes. Big corporate companies are willing to write a sponsorship check even if it's your first event. Don't make excuses and cause disbelief. I've had banks donate $12K and soft drink companies donate $50K to first time events. They saw a new opportunity to reach a new audience. . Pick a niche and go after the companies that align with your mission. For example, if your organization is in the mental health market, focus on sending sponsorship packages to hospitals, rehabilitation and recovery centers, doctors, banks, insurance companies, and pharmacies. If your organization helps women, focus on organizations that empower women. You can create a free user profile on Hunter. io and search for global alliance mangers who's responsibilities include giving money away.

#2. It's important to scrape old lists and weed out people who have moved, passed away or no longer contribute to your cause. Buying several business lists of potential sponsorships each year is highly recommended. These business lists are sold by categories and listed by industry. The listings are very affordable and easily accessible through the Albany Business Review Book of List. - 40 British American Blvd. Albany, NY 12110 (518)-640-6800. You can also Google other business trade newspapers and ask if they sell business lists. Once you buy a few new business listings, you can begin to update and merge. Use email marketing tools such as Constant Contact, Mail Chimp, or Actionetics through Click Funnels to send email marketing and opportunities every two weeks. You can also create a Chatbot using ManyChat.com to increase engagement via Facebook Messenger bots.

#3. Increase volunteers, donors and sponsors with using the cutting edge technology of Click Funnels, the world's premier online sales and marketing software, to make it easy to do (no coders, developers, or computer wizards needed).

Create a Click Funnels account and start building a list of supporters and sponsors. Try it for Free! Here's the link for a free 14 day trial of Click Funnels bit.ly/Maya14DayFreeTrialCF

Click Funnels software can measure list growth success for your nonprofit using Actionetics. Click Funnels software helps users grow their businesses or nonprofit. The innovative software design simplifies and saves you money and time when it comes to hiring a tech team, program coder, graphic designer, website developer and handles all the techy complicated stuff. Click Funnels easy to use software platform is helping to revolutionize the future of online marketing.

Today funnels are one of the best ways to communicate your audience because you can connect to people anywhere the world. You also own this list and can market offers whenever a new opportunity arises at no added cost. The more qualified subscriber's contacts your organization curates, the better open rate your email marketing campaign will have. You'll also have a better chance of enticing people to do business with you. That's why it's important to continuously grow your list. Chatbots are another effective and efficient tool you can use to grow your subscriber list. Go to ManyChat.com to create an account. Understanding what works and what doesn't will allow you to improve your results. Using Click Funnels software will help to calculate list growth and put new subscribers into buckets so that you can test different offers and sign- up methods. Your list metrics should automate regularly so you can see the rate of the list growth in real time. This method tracks your unsubscribe rate as well.

Once your list begins to grow, you'll have an abundance of qualified leads. By following up and being consistent, your new list will have a higher engagement with your organization.

Secret Tip #4 Create Your Free 14 day Click Funnels account. Grow your list.

Secret #12 Be Social

Creating dozens of social media pages or handles is not necessary. First, it's way too time consuming and difficult to manage. Having too many social media accounts can be overwhelming especially, if you have a small staff and no marketing department. Finding the right social media handle that works for your organization and staff can be tricky. The best advice I can share is to create a social media handle that you like using. Narrow in on a few platforms your team enjoys using and with which your donors and supporters feel comfortable engaging. For example, if your target audience is 18-35, they are probably on Twitter, Snap Chat and Instagram. If your audience is 25-95 you'll find them on Facebook. You Tube is a great place to advertise and drive traffic to your Click Funnels account or donation link. You can use scheduling applications such as Hootsuite to schedule postings. I will warn however, scheduling tools have lower engagement on Facebook's post. It's common sense that people like to do business with people. The engagement has to be done by a person manually in house or hire an agency that specializes in social media handles. LinkedIn is a free platform and is often overlooked as a source for leads. LinkedIn is an excellent source for potential leads and donors. Shapr is a free app to collaborate and find leads. Your organization should decide on at least 3 social platforms to continue and participate in the conversation, and build your trust with the audience. Once you've established trust, create an events page and invite your new tribe of supporters to join in and build a Cult-ure around this new congregation. Continue the conversation on your business page or group page. Invite local community leaders and volunteers to collaborate and support your mission.

Personally, I enjoy engaging with Facebook. I find it easiest and fun. Below are 5 Tips for Making Facebook Live Videos Better. Facebook Live is the #1 way to get in front of your audience. These Live videos connect you to real people. In addition, show that you care and solve a problem. When I was volunteering my time at the City Mission feeding the hungry, I could feel along with see the emotional connection. People like to do business with people. People also donate to people. This is why Facebook Lives is better than recorded videos and static images.

5 Tips For Making Facebook Live Vi

Better

1. What to say to increase engagement:

- Ask for Likes, Shares, Hearts and Thumbs Up
- Call out your viewers by name
- Ask for #replay on the replay
- Ask people where they're from
- Mention to the later broadcast viewers to comment
- Most of the views will occur after the initial live, so keep asking for the engagement
- Have a topic of value to talk about or teach
- Introduce yourself
- Tell them what your Topic is tomorrow – but use Cliffhangers

(This will boost your engagement and Facebook will show your post longer.)

2. Correct position to hold your phone:

- Your phone screen is expensive Real Estate. Holding your phone vertically is best for Facebook engagement. A vertical hold will show your face and upper body. When scrolling through Facebook your vertical post will take up more space. The only problem with holding your phone vertically is that you'll get the black lines on both sides of your repurposed videos should you choose to use on YouTube. The vertical hold is also great for Instagram and Insta stories. To avoid the black strips on both sides of my videos, I like to hold my phone horizontally. By holding the phone horizontally you do take up less real estate on the Facebook scroll resulting in lower engagement. Your video can also be repurposed in your Funnel or YouTube and other video sites.

3. Have a Good Title:

- "How to" or "5 Tips" videos rank higher for title reach and engagement. You can research Free Headlines and Best Titles using the analyzer. This free tool will analyze your headline to determine the emotional marketing value (EMV) score.

Website: www.Aminstitute.Com/headlines

4. Have good lighting:

- To increase engagement, good lighting is key when doing Facebook live videos. For under $8 you can purchase ring lights on Amazon. Sitting by a window or lamp will bring natural light to your videos. Soft boxes are also a great solution as well.

5. Have Fun!

- Be fun to watch. Be engaging. Call viewers by name. Ask for the engagement. A good length of time for a Facebook Live is 15-18 minutes.

Bonus tip: Have a Call to Action. Be clear and ask for the sale, share or donation. Be clear with your Call to Action

- Join my Group
- Buy my Course
- Download my Guide

Use this helpful and simple checklist to elevate your Facebook fan page.

✓ Is your website listed in your "About" section?
✓ Does your profile image reflect your brand?
✓ Do you have an eye- catching cover photo?
✓ Is your website address in the description of your cover photo?
✓ Did you include your other social media links in the additional "About" section?
✓ Do you have apps, with call to action?
✓ Are you sharing eye catching images?
✓ Are you sharing your videos?
✓ Are you doing Facebook Lives on your fan page?
✓ Are you liking and commenting back with your fans?
✓ Are you posting at least 5 times a week?
✓ Are you sharing other pages post?
✓ Are you tagging other businesses and people?
✓ Is your events calendar filled out?
✓ Do you have interesting photo albums?

Secret Tip # 5 Be Engaging and Social on Social Media.

Secret #12 Ask for Help

Let's be real! It's usually our egos and pride that gets in our way of asking for help. Your tribe wants to help you to succeed. You just have to ask. Most organizations are comprised of a small staff and solely rely on volunteers. Not all volunteers are good for your nonprofit. Listen to my podcast Fundraising Secrets on Apple Podcast, Itunes, Google Play, Podbean, Cashbox, Spotify, Stitcher, Anchor.fm etc., and learn why you need to have a volunteer job description in place.

When creating an event, collaborate with local community leaders and encourage them to volunteer with your organization. Form partnerships with other nonprofits, and collaborate with local businesses for in kind services, contributions, donations of products and services. Continue the conversations weekly.

Prepare a spreadsheet similar to a cadency report. Do this spreadsheet in Excel or Google docs so you can easily share with the Steering Committee, volunteers and staff, all progress points of campaign or event. When the volunteers feel included, they become fueled with desire to fight for the cause and champion the mission. In the documents, ask for permission to include emails, and phone numbers of event contributors for further and consistent communication throughout the campaign. It is vital that all communication be done weekly, clearly and consistently to ensure a vibrant team of volunteers and donors.

This is also a great time to delegate responsibilities amongst the Steering Committee, Board Members, Planning Committee, and Volunteers. By referencing your value ladder delegating task should be seamless and keep your team in momentum as your conquering important tasks.

Secret #13 How To Eat An Elephant

It's extremely easy to become overwhelmed with project deadlines. The question is, how do you eat an elephant? The correct answer is one piece at a time. In the beginning the project task will feel as if you're pushing a boulder up a mountain. If you like pie, it's like shoving a whole pie in your mouth at once. You'll choke. You might even get sick. This is where you'd call on your team. It will be to your best advantage to communicate with the Steering Committee and agree on important dates and deadlines ahead of time. After nailing down concrete dates, stick to them by creating a timeline. Do not waver. This process will alleviate tons of stress and keep the team in momentum. Some important dates to nail down straight away include the event date, time and location, bi- weekly Steering Committee meetings as well as the Meet and Greet party date, time and venue for all the volunteers and community leaders. Next will be the Recap and Thank You Party date, time and venue. This will ensure that all event steps are met and no stone goes unturned. Other important dates to schedule will be the final debriefing meeting with the Steering Committee one week after the event.

A debriefing report should be prepared and submitted to all Steering Committee members, Broad Members and President of the organization. This will summarize the fundraising and close out the fiscal event.

Also, a final evaluation/ analysis letter should be submitted from the Steering Committee and presented to the President and Board Members.

Meeting Minutes Example:

Special Olympics New York Runway for the Gold Steering Committee Meeting

Tuesday, May 8, 2018

Minutes

I. <u>Call to Order:</u> The meeting was called to order at 9:11 a.m. by Chair Maya McNulty at Panera Breads, Niskayuna.

II. <u>Roll Call:</u> Present: Jon Doe, Maya McNulty, Melissa O'Reilly and Wilma Schmeler.

III. <u>Approval of April 9, 2018 Committee Meeting Minutes</u>: It was moved by Melissa O' Reilly and seconded by Maya McNulty that the minutes of the 04-09-18 meeting be approved. Carried.

IV. <u>Comprehensive Financial Report:</u>

Jon presented his report. Copies are attached to these minutes on file.

<u>Summary for 2018 as of 05-08-18</u>:

- Revenue:
  o Sponsorships: $11,500: (Coca-Cola-$5,000; Regeneron-$2,000; Denooyer Chevrolet-$1,500; Frank&Wilma Schmeler-$1,000; Smith Family-$1,000; Primaloft-$1,000)
  o Model Fundraising: $23,716
  o Ticket sales: $3,800. – 62
  o Sponsor an Athlete/50-50/Silent Auction: $4,000
  o General Donations: $125

Total Income: <u>$43,141</u>

- <u>Expenses:</u>

o To date, <u>$8,246</u> of our $10K budget has been spent:(Emcee-$300; DJ-$300; Fondue/Smile Monster-$225; Venue-$5,078; Stage-$775; Save the Dates-$400; Invitations-$700; Medals-$68; Misc Printing, Décor etc.-$400)
- <u>Net Profit:$34,895</u>

V. <u>05-04-18 – Re-Cap Party:</u>

- A great time was had by all who attended the party at Katie O'Byrne's Irish Pub & Restaurant in Schenectady. Party was 'gifted' by the owners.
- Maya welcomed everyone and thanked all who helped with the success of 'Runway for the Gold'. Maya's 'script' is attached to the original minutes on file. Janet Jones response to Maya: "It's been a wonderful night and your message was inspiring, Maya".

VI. <u>De-brief/Evaluation/Feedback – Runway for the Gold Fashion Show</u>

- Feedback &Survey Monkey results:
o Too many models
o More make-up artists and hair stylists needed
o Emcees were not well rehearsed
o Sound-DJ overpowered emcees
o Not enough recognition to vendors, donors, sponsors
o Program well paced
o Sponsor-an-Athlete well received
o Longer intermission needed
o Great enthusiasm and audience participation
o Program booklet well done
o Excellent venue, food and service
o Registration and welcome well done.
o Silent Auction - adequate

VII. <u>Recommendations for next year – to SONY CEO</u>

- Wilma presented her document: 'Runway for the Gold 2018 – Evaluation/Analysis'. This was reviewed and edited. On behalf of the Steering Committee, Wilma will submit this edited document to Janet Jones, President & CEO – Special Olympics New York.

VIII. <u>Closure on Runway for the Gold - 2018:</u>

- Thank you letters – should be sent to all who helped with the success of RWFTG if they haven't already been sent a formal 'thank you' letter.

IX. <u>Next Meeting Date:</u>

- None scheduled

X. <u>Adjournment:</u>

- Jon Doe moved the adjournment of the meeting at 10:15 a.m.

Respectfully submitted,

Wilma Schmeler, Recorder

June 5, 2018

| Secret Tip #6 Schedule important dates in advance.

Secret #14 Checklist

Before a pilot takes off in his plane, he checks his safety checklist. Even if he's flown a hundred times before or is on a one hour layover from a short flight he rechecks his checklist 2 or 3 times before taking off again. He's also dressed for the role of a pilot and commands respect and authority. The pilot then greets his co-pilot, flight crew and passengers. He'll check to makes sure that the plane has enough fuel and that the gears, wings and landing wheels work. He'll also, make sure the doors are locked and emergency kits and doors can be found in case of an emergency before taking off to his scheduled destination. The pilot has a system that ensures the safety of his team, passengers and plane. Because of the pilot safety checklist, no step is ever missed or overlooked. A checklist provides a proven system and peace of mind so that you will arrive safely and allows the pilot to fly his plane confidently and without distractions.

A check list is just as important for your event as it is for the pilot. I'd recommend creating 2 checklists. One for the day before the event to make sure you have everything in place so that you're not running around crazy looking for things. Start crossing off the checklist items and put them in the car/truck you will be driving to the event the night before. If you have more than one vehicle mention to your teenage kids and husband not take your car or empty your car out. I've had this happen to me.

Create a second checklist for the day of the event. For example, if you have outside food, flowers or auction items that needs to be picked up. You'll want to have a second checklist to knock off items. Remember that, you're racing against the clock. Make every minute count. The second checklist is a recap checklist of the first one. Plus any pertinent information, such as program booklets, plaques, balloons, batteries, pins, step and repeats signage, DJ and Emcee scripts, flags, photos, up lighting, auction sheets, volunteer thank you sheets, 50/50 tickets, sponsor video, stage and microphone setup and tested, credit card processor, checks payments for venue and hired help.

As the hours move closer to the event, it's easy to become distracted. Someone will have a last minute request. A checklist will help to avoid chaos and make the event run smoothly and efficiently. Don't get trapped and be disorganized minutes before your event. I promise you that an effective checklist will become your saving grace.

Secret #15 Postal Permits

This entry was a conversation with Jeff Leverett, Post Master at the US Postal Service on Tuesday, November 6, 2018. (You can listen to the full Episode 12, Fundraising Secrets Podcast on Apple Podcast, Itunes, Stitcher, Anchor.fm, Spotify, Castbox, Podbean and Droid.)

Originally, I couldn't decide if postal permits would be of value. Jeff confirmed it was important and indeed valuable. I spoke with Jeff at length. He explained the step by step process to acquiring a nonprofit permit through the US Postal Service. He also gave insight as to how anyone can apply for a nonprofit permit.

Jeff was extremely knowledgeable, kind and enthusiastic about sharing his postal policies and procedures. When I shared exactly what I was doing, Jeff became even more engaged and excited. I was completely transparent with Jeff. I let him in on the secret of my inquiry. I mentioned that I'm actually not really calling about finding out about permits, but I'm calling because I need to learn about permits for the book I'm writing called *Fundraising Secrets*. I asked Jeff if he thinks this content might be of interest and importance.

Jeff started to chuckle as he became more transparent and explained the exact process. It's actually a lengthy process he warned. With candor Jeff mentioned that's probably one of the main reasons why many nonprofits don't have a permit for their organization. Jeff went into more details. There's little ways around permit fees and regulations that perhaps you'll find value in getting a permit or not getting a permit or using a mail house for your permits.

Jeff had a couple of suggestions. One is y
permit, and it's a process. Only nonprofits a
commercial use are authorized. Nonprofit
discount, a discounted rate from the comm
are some steps, and you have to identify you.
You have to go through this process listed below.

For example, a regular customer, a commercial customer, has
an annual application fee of $225 applies to you to be able to
register your permit. There's another application fee. This is a
one-time application fee for $225 and that will open your permit.
You can use that for commercial use. The commercial business
permit takes twenty minutes to process. You must show two
forms of identifications as part of the requirements.

As a nonprofit the process is a little bit more complex. The two
step permit process allows the ability of sending your mailings
at a discounted rate and link to your nonprofit permit status.
The two step nonprofit permit is a free application making it
easy to apply. You can visit any US Postal Service and easily
apply and submit forms.

Another alternative is doing a mailing in-house and not use a
mail house. You have the ability to open a permit, and you would
be paying $225. It's an annual fee, and then there's a one– time
application fee of $225. There's two parts for mailing in house.

Let's say that you're a nonprofit, and you don't want to get your
own permit in-house and use a commercial house to be able to
do your permit and mailings. Here's a couple of permit houses
that Jeff suggested.

These mailing houses include, Digital Express, Mailworks,
Velocity, and Centron. I personally like Nielsen Associates
1-800-230-3256 www.mailprep.com

Now if a nonprofit chooses to use a mail house, they only need
to apply for a free authorization, free application for nonprofits.
You'll save $450. This way you can be off to mailing your
business mail and your information in a timely manner.

if your organization is struggling to find volunteers and have a small staff, the mail house would actually help to alleviate the pressure. The mail houses, organizes and get your pieces to the right size and the right weight. They do all the work for you. Imagine saving $450, saving a lot of time, especially if your organization is smaller, and extend your reach to a larger audience.

Now, if you're considering going through the process of getting your permit and then also your free nonprofit permit, follow these 3 short steps. You must follow exact in order to proceed as a legitimate non – profit. Step 1, you must provide a letter from the IRS showing proof of articles of incorporation. Step 2, you must have proof validating that you're in operations. Step 3, you need newsletters, monthly tax records, tax records, mailings, meeting minutes, things to show that you are a corporation providing names on the documents, showing proof that you have established your corporation.

An extremely important part of the nonprofit permit regulations is your permit stamp. When you are applying for your permit, you must have your stamp on your return address labels, and on your application, those articles of incorporation and the letters from the IRS have to match your name exactly. The name can't read MM nonprofit if your application is register to Maya McNulty nonprofit. It has to be Maya McNulty nonprofit. It has to match all documents exactly all of the time. Exactly what your application said on your IRS forms and articles of incorporation and your proof of operation. There can't be any abbreviations, or your permit will be denied and then you'll have to pay the normal commercial rate. Make sure that your name is spelled exactly as registered and have everything matching correctly.

Another reason mailing houses are great resources is because they do all the transporting and all the sizing and heavy lifting so it saves a ton of valuable time.

The free nonprofit permit application will save you $450. But if you want to do it in- house, its $225 annual fee and then a one-time application fee of $225 additional.

Once you get your application approved, it's a good idea to document dates for permit renewal. You'll need to provide two forms of ID for renewal. They will accept your driver license or a passport and another picture ID such as, a credit card with a picture. Other forms of ID needed include mailing from your bank and something else showing proof of your nonprofit business.

There are different permit classes as well. There's first class and standard class. In each class your mailings will hold different rates for you to be able to send your information out.

As stated, the procedure for getting a nonprofit status is free. All you have to do is apply. You can get your mailing down to as cheap as 12 cents or less depending on what you're mailing. You have to submit proof of your articles of incorporation and other things to be granted the authorization. When you rent someone else's mail house, your nonprofit stamp must show proof and name spelled correctly to avoid being charged the regular commercial postage rate.

Just a final note from Jeff, he mentioned, "I've seen a lot of nonprofits that come into the post office and a lot of them struggle with name clarity. In fact, there was one that was over 150 years old that came in and they had to deny them their permit status because things didn't match."

Secret Tip #7 Verify that nonprofit name is spelled correctly and matches all documents.

Chapter Three:

Sponsorship Proposal Secrets

Funding is the oxygen for staying alive. This is true for any business. Many businesses and nonprofits struggle to find resources and funding to champion their mission. Becoming more resourceful compares to a heartbeat. If there is a pulse, there is hope.

Sponsorship Secrets will save your organization's life. Just follow the step by step blueprint and you will have checks arriving in your mailbox daily. Listen to **Episode #47: Be The Change & Stop The Stigma Surrounding Mental Illness with NAMI** on Fundraising Secrets Podcast. The NAMI- Directors Matthew Shapiro and Tina Lee speak on funding and raising $43K in under 8 weeks. It's an excellent episode.

In my opinion, here are a few reasons why sponsorship Ask often fail to convert.

12 Reasons Why Sponsorship ASK Fail:

1. The organization didn't ask for enough money
2. The stack offer wasn't creative or favorable to the sponsor
3. The nonprofit failed to follow up
4. Bad timing of the year
5. The donor is no longer vested in the relationship with the organization
6. The nonprofit failed to appropriately thank the sponsor in the past
7. The nonprofit didn't fulfill promise on past sponsorships
8. The sponsorship deadline wasn't reasonable
9. The organization's political views
10. The organization failed to ask different departments within a huge corporation

11. Nonprofit failed to build a relationship
12. The donor died

The good news is this can be easily corrected. As you begin to draw out your offer on a white board of your sponsorship package be creative. Straight up, Ask for more money. Create an attractive offer by adding more value. Send out sponsorship timely and Follow Up! Remember to thank your sponsors more than once, be polarizing, but not political. Be transparent and honest with your sponsors by over delivering on your promise. Send sponsorship ask letters to different departments. This will greatly increase your sponsorship relationship. Begin to build relationships by connecting with your sponsors via Zoom or Skype. A face to face or belly to belly connection will convert higher.

When planning an event the best practices for the organization would be to prepare a list of prospective sponsors 4-6 months in advance of the event. Sponsorship is a great way to collaborate with corporate organizations and other community businesses. Secret #16 revels several ways to insure your sponsorship proposal gets past the gate keeper, reaches the decision maker and not the maintenance man.

Secret # 16 Create an Attractive Offer

While there is no one size fits all for designing a sponsorship proposal there are few basic elements that should be included:

- A cover letter
- A cover page
- A positioning statement
- A list of benefits
- A list of key contacts
- Testimonials
- Offer Pricing

Your cover letter should be customized to the sponsor. You need to engage them quickly by highlighting points that will get them excited and interested in learning more.

Don't overload your potential sponsor with lots of information. Instead, keep it simple with a brief introduction and a focus on the potential outcomes for the SPONSOR – not what's in it for the organization.

An effective sponsorship package has these six things in this order to get your feet in the door.

1. Who
2. What
3. Where
4. Why
5. How
6. Creative Sponsorship Ask

Let's break it down.

➢ Who are you?

➢ What is it?

➢ Where is the event?

➢ Why people should attend.

➢ How can they support.

These six (6) steps in Sponsorship Secrets work. Improve the offer for the Sponsor and you will secure higher conversion rate.

Example of Sponsorship Letter on Letterhead:

National Alliance on Mental Illness

December 17, 2018

Dear Mary James,

Every year, regardless of race, age, religion, or economic status, mental illness impacts the lives of at least 1 in 4 Adults and 1 in 5 children across the United States. Unfortunately, stigma is still the leading cause to why people fail to seek help. Increasing mental health literacy, awareness, and outreach in our communities can have a tremendous ripple effect, and you can be a part of the solution.

WHO

NAMI-NYS is the state chapter of the National Alliance on Mental Illness (NAMI), the nation's largest, 501 (c)(3), grassroots organization dedicated to improving the lives of people living with mental illness. For over 35 years, NAMI-NYS has effectively provided and connected families, individuals, schools, and families of veterans with resources, support, free education, and advocacy to maintain vibrant and mentally healthy communities across New York State.

WHAT

WHERE

I am asking you to join us as a sponsor to end the silence and stigma and raise awareness about the importance of mental wellness in your community at our *Off The Mask Fashion Show and Art Exhibit* on Friday, May, 10, 2019 from 6:00 pm to 9:00 p.m. at The Hearst Media Center, 645 Albany Shaker Road, Albany NY. The evening agenda will include a cocktail party, fashion show, a silent auction, and a juried art show. Over 300 prominent business, civic, and community leaders will gather at the benefit to celebrate our collaborative efforts and showcase the strength, heart, and soul of our organization. Our goal is to raise $65,000 to help fund our FREE programs that change attitudes and save lives.

WHY

As a sponsor, you can help redefine the narrative on mental health. The enclosed materials provide details about our sponsorship opportunities. We also welcome monetary donations and silent auction items. All donations will be recognized in our program book, electronic journal, auction table, social media platform with over 3,000 followers, weekly electronic newsletter with over 10,000 subscribers, and website. **Sponsorship commitments must be made by Monday, March 4, 2019.**

For more information, please visit our event website at: OffTheMask.org or contact Tina Lee, Community Education and Outreach Manager by email: Tina@naminys.org or 518-462-2000, x 106.

We thank you in advance for giving the gift of Hope and Recovery.

Sincerely,

Wendy Burch
Executive Director, NAMI-NYS

Maya McNulty
Off The Mask Steering Committee

99 Pine Street, Suite 105 Albany, New York 12207   Phone: (518) 462-2000 or (800) 950-3228 (NY only)   Fax: (518) 462-3811
Email: info@naminys.org Helpline: helpline@naminys.org Website: www.naminys.org

It would be to the organization's best advantage to craft the sponsorship offer at least 2-3 weeks in advance and be creative. I'd recommend not copying sponsorships from Google or using the traditional Red, Blue, Gold and Platinum ask. Be creative and show originality emphasizing your organization's mission. You'll notice below the different levels of sponsorship listed, **Hope, Inspire, Wellness and Recovery.** This is the language used by NAMI and the sponsors both can visualize and feel the mission. By creating an attractive offer the sponsorship package will peak curiosity of the each sponsor. An example of Duel Sponsorship is listed as a reference. This is an excellent opportunity for both sponsor and the organization. The more irresistible the offer the better your chances are for securing sponsorships. If your organization hosts more than one event per year this is a great opportunity to get your feet in the door, piggy back off each event and give more value to the sponsors. They will see the value you bring. Remember to include a sponsorship response form along with sponsorship online options. Make it easy for the sponsor to contribute to your organization.

Another thing you can do to add more value to your sponsorship package is add a personalized letter or note from a board member or volunteer. This method speaks volumes because people are busy and don't often take the time to write hand written notes. The sponsor will find this special touch appealing.

Secret #17 Follow -Up

Where most businesses fail is in the Follow – Up. If you've ever heard the fortune is in the follow up, it's true. Follow – up, Follow-up, Follow- up!! The "Cash" is for "Closers" by following up you will acquire droves of new sponsorships. The old way to follow up is by picking up the phone and calling or sending emails. The best practice for getting higher ticket sponsors is connecting with the donor on Skype, Facetime, Zoom or Free Conference Call.com. You can find specific people and their departments on the website Hunter.io

You will want to create a free profile on Hunter.io and start connecting with key influencers. The people to reach out to include: Brand Managers, Global Alliance Managers, Community Outreach, and Community Development. You will want to send an initial email with a killer headline, a warm but brief introduction and an invitation to connect on Skype, Facetime, Zoom, or Free Conference Call. Begin to build the relationship with your first few interactions before you do any ask. You will want to have your sponsorship proposal ready in case the conversation leads to that opportunity. A sponsorship proposal should be unique and less than 10 pages.

Example of Sponsorship Opportunities:

OFF THE MASK

Friday, May 10, 2019 * Hearst MediaCenter * 645 Albany Hearst ShakerRoadAlbanyNY
6:00 pm - 9:00 pm
FashionShow* CocktailParty * JuriedArtExhibit* SilentAuction

The National Alliance on Mental Illness New York State (NAMI-NYS) provides FREE and confidential education and supports to families and individuals impacted by mental illness.

We hope that we can count on you to ChangeAttitudesand SaveLives!

Sponsorship Opportunities

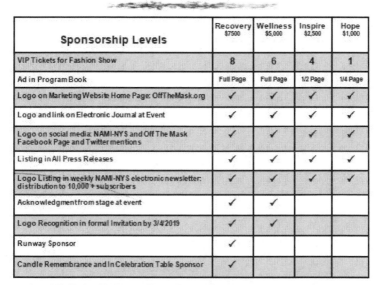

Sponsorship Levels	Recovery $7500	Wellness $5,000	Inspire $2,500	Hope $1,000
VIP Tickets for Fashion Show	8	6	4	1
Ad in Program Book	Full Page	Full Page	1/2 Page	1/4 Page
Logo on Marketing Website Home Page: OffTheMask.org	✓	✓	✓	✓
Logo and link on Electronic Journal at Event	✓	✓	✓	✓
Logo on social media: NAMI-NYS and Off The Mask Facebook Page and Twitter mentions	✓	✓	✓	✓
Listing in All Press Releases	✓	✓	✓	✓
Logo Listing in weekly NAMI-NYS electronic newsletter: distribution to 10,000 + subscribers	✓	✓	✓	✓
Acknowledgment from stage at event	✓	✓		
Logo Recognition in formal Invitation by 3/4/2019	✓	✓		
Runway Sponsor	✓			
Candle Remembrance and In Celebration Table Sponsor	✓			

The National Alliance on Mental Illness New York State (NAMI-NYS) Mission:
NAMI-NYS is dedicated to the support and education of families and individuals living with serious and persistent brain disorders (mental illness). NAMI-NYS advocates for better services in the public system of care, seeks to educate the public about the myths of mental illness to eradicate stigma, and supports brain research.

For more information on Off TheMask, please contact:
Tina Lee, Community Education and Outreach Manager, NAMI-NYS: Tina @naminys.org, 518-462-2000 x 106

Example of Duel Sponsorship Opportunities:

DualSponsorshipOpportunities

OfftheMask Friday, May 10, 2019 Hearst Media Center 645 Albany Shaker Road, Albany NY 6:00 pm - 9:00 pm	NAMI-NYS EducationConference October 25th-27th, 2019 Marriott Hotel 189 Wolf Road, Albany NY

Dual Sponsorship Levels	Platinum $10,000	Gold $7,500	Silver $5,000	Bronze $2,500
Off The Mask Sponsorship Opportunities	Recovery Sponsorship Plus	Wellness Sponsorship Plus	Inspire Sponsorship Plus	Hope Sponsorship Plus
Ad in NAMI-NYS Education Conference Program Book	Full Color Page	Full B-W Page	Full B-W Page	1/2 B-W Page
LogoonNAMI-NYSEducationConferenceWebsite	✓	✓	✓	✓
Logo on social media: NAMI-NYS Facebook page and twitter mentions	✓	✓	✓	✓
Listing in All Press Releases	✓	✓	✓	✓
Public Acknowledgment on Friday Night NAMI-NYS Education Conference Dinner	✓	✓	✓	✓
Table for Ten (10) at NAMI-NYS Education Conference Friday Night Dinner	✓	✓		
10' x 10' Exhibit Space at NAMI-NYS Education Conference	✓	✓	✓	✓
Materials in NAMI-NYS Education Conference bags if provided	✓	✓		
VIP Reception Invitation for NAMI-NYS Education Conference Friday Night Dinner	✓	✓	✓	✓
Registration for NAMI-NYS Education Conference	10	5	4	2

For more information on NAMI-NYS Education Conference, please contact:
Matthew Shapiro, Associate Director Public Affairs NAMI-NYS: Matthew@naminys.org, 518-462-2000 x 108

Example of Sponsorship Signature Form:

SponsorCommitmentForm

Name:				
(as you wish it to appear on event materials)				
Address:	City:		State:	Zip:
Contact Person:				
Email:		Phone: ( ) -		

Sponsor Level: (Please check One)	Payment Method: (Please check appropriate boxes.)
	☒ Check (Made payable to: NAMI-NYS)
	☐ Mastercard ☐ Visa ☐ American Express ☐ Discover
Recovery $7,500	Credit Card #: CVC:
Wellness $5,000	Cardholder Name:
Inspire $2,500	Billing Address: Zip Code:
Hope $1,000	Authorized Signature: _____

ImportantDeadlineandInformation:

* Formal Invitation: To be included on the invitation, sponsorship pledge and company logo must be received by Monday, March 4, 2019.

* Event Program Booklet: To be included in the Event Program Booklet, sponsorship pledge and company ad must be received by: Tuesday, March 26, 2019.

AdSpecs: AcceptableFormatsinclude: PDF, EPS, JPG
FullPage: 8" hx 5"w
HalfPage: 4" hx 5" w
QuarterPage: 2" hx 5" w

OFF THE MASK

PleasereturnthisformbyMonday, March 4, 2019to:

Tina@naminys.org or Attn:Tina Lee, NAMI-NYS, 99 PineStreet, Suite 105 AlbanyNY 12207

Ads and Logos: email to: Tina@naminys.org

RegistrationandSponsorshipAvailableonlineat: OffTheMask.org

For more information, please contact: Tina Lee at (518) 462-2000 x 106 or tina@naminys.org
Friday, May 10, 2019 * 6:00 pm - 9:00 pm * Hearst Media Center * 645 Albany Shaker Road Albany NY

Example of Silent Auction Donation Form:

OFF THE MASK

Silent Auction Donation

Friday, May 10, 2019 * HearstMediaCenter * 645 AlbanyShakerRoadAlbanyNY
6:00 pm - 9:00 pm

Fashion Show* CocktailParty * JuriedArtExhibit* SilentAuction

Donor Name:			
(as you wish it to appe aro nevenf material s)			
Organization or Business:		Website:	
Address:	City:		State:
Contact Person:			
Phone No.( ) - -	Email:		
Item or Service Description (Please use a separate form for each donation.)			
Fair Market Value of Item Donated: $			
☐ Item is a service. I have enclosed a certificate for the service to be provided. ☐ Item needs to be picked up.			
Address: (if different from above.)	City:		State:
☐ Item will be delivered/shipped in advance to: Attn: Tina,NAMI-NYS, 99 Pine Street, Ste. 105, Albany NY 12207			

In order for your donation will be included in the program booklet,
you must submit your Silent Auction Donation by: **March 26, 2019.**

This receipt serves as acknowledgment of your donation of the item(s) listed above to **Off The Mask** Fashion Show and Art Exhibit tobenefit NAMI-NYS. Contributions of goods are deductible forincome tax purposes to the extent allowed by law. Estimating the fair market value of in-kind donations is the privilege and responsibility of the donor. NAMI-NYS **Off The Mask** has provided no goods or services in consideration of this donation.

Donor Signature:	Date: / /

Please email this form to: tina@naminys.org or fax: (518) 462-3811.

We thank you in advance for ChangingAttitudes and SavingLives!
Proceeds will go toward our FREE and confidential programming and supports
to families and individuals impacted by mental illness.

NAMI has an "A" rating from the AmericanInstitute of Philanthropy and was ranked by *Worth*magazine in its Top
100 Charities as "most likely to save the World."
NAMI has also received the BBB seal (Better Business Bureau)
forexcellent standards for charity accountability.

Secret #18 Calling Script

A well written calling script is necessary during the follow up process. Prepare a calling script for volunteers and members of your dream team that will engage your niche. Fundraising is the job of the entire organization. Everyone should be aware and taking part in the asking for donations. This calling script should be used when following up on emails, letters or phone calls.

Example of Volunteer Calling Script to Donor:

Calling Script - 'Runway for the Gold' Donor Sponsor Prospects

Hello _____,

This is _____, a volunteer at Special Olympics New York, calling. I am reaching out to you to follow up on the letter you recently received inviting you to sponsor Special Olympics New York's 2nd Annual Runway for the Gold Fashion Show and Cocktail Party which will be held on Thursday, April 12that 6 o'clock at the Mohawk River Country Club in Rexford, New York.

Our Special Olympic athletes will proudly catwalk down the Runway with community leaders showing us what they have accomplished. It promises to be an enjoyable evening of camaraderie in support of our Special Olympic athletes who are competing in this year's 50th Special Olympics New York Summer Games at Siena College in June.

Please support our athletes by sponsoring the 'Runway for the Gold'. Your support will ensure that all of our athletes have the opportunity to compete in one of the most important competitions of their lifetime at no cost to them, their families or caregivers.

Sponsorship levels, benefits and timelines are described in the information you received a few weeks ago. If you need additional information we can email it to you or please contact Jim Carrie at (518) 388-0790 or Jcarrie@nyso.org Registration and Sponsorship is also available online: www.runwayforthegold.org

Please note that registration for Sponsorships is due February 9th so that we can meet our printing deadline.

Thank you for considering this request, and we hope we can count on you to support and champion our Special Olympic athletes as they compete in the upcoming Special Olympics New York Summer Games at Siena College.

Again, it's _____ calling on behalf of our Special Olympics New York athletes.

THANK YOU!!!

_____

_____

Please note:

- This is a "suggested" calling script. Use it, modify it, or just use your own words. The important thing to say up front is that you are a volunteer for Special Olympics New York.... This usually quickly relaxes people and makes them open to the reason for your call.
- For additional information that you may want to mention, please refer to the 'Letter of Invitation' and 'Brochure' that all sponsorship prospects have received.

Secret 19 Click Funnels

In Secret 11 we revealed the power of Click Funnels. Click Funnels is technology software that Co- Founders and Owners Russell Brunson and Todd Dickerson developed to revolutionize the way businesses and nonprofits generate traffic and succeed. Every business needs a funnel. Period.

Click Funnels is a simple tool used to automate the process of getting qualified leads, donors, and businesses to do business with you. The concept of a funnel targets your ideal customer or client without you doing any extra heavy lifting. If your organization has a small team and small donor base, Click Funnels is right for you.

Create a Click Funnels account and start building a list of supporters and sponsors. Try it for Free! Here's the link for a free 14 day trail of Click Funnels.

Get Click Funnels: http://bit.ly/Maya14DayFreeTrialCF

I would also recommend ordering your free copy of *Expert Secrets* and *Dot Com Secrets* to help guide along. (Just pay shipping.)

These two books will extract your organizations stories and help you to connect with your congregation quickly.

Get Expert Secrets Here: http://bit.ly/MayaExpertSecretsBook

Get *Dot Com Secrets* Here: http://bit.ly/MayaDotComSecrets

Two BONUS training courses: Learn How to Build a Funnel for your nonprofit in 30 days. http://bit.ly/Mayaonefunnelaway

Learn How to Fundraise Fast 30 Day Challenge www.fundraisefast.com

Secret 20 How to Avoid High Bank Fees

You're not alone. We all feel the sting from high bank fees. It's even harder to swallow if you're a nonprofit because you're counting every penny to champion your mission. Every business owner is trying to cut expenses especially when it comes to high bank fees. The banking industry is a very competitive market. As more and more nonprofits compete for the same dollars they are searching for better ways to lower their credit card rate so that they can retain their donations. Free donation tools such as donor box have plug in widget to help nonprofits with donations. Organizations can register for a free account at www.donorbox.org

After you become a member of Click Funnels, your organization can set up a free Stripe Account www.stripe.com Stripe has no fees and 100% of the donations is deposited into your Stripe Account and later transferred into your business account. It's a great option for international donations as well.

Paypal has become extremely popular with nonprofits for collecting donations. The transaction fee is lower. Your organization can take donations online or mobile driven. You will avoid high merchant leasing fees, bank fees and credit card processing fees. Create a free Paypal.me account at Paypal.com

Traditionally, nonprofits have been receiving donor checks in the mail. This is all going to change as the world progresses into a mobile internet and paperless society. Using the Free tools listed above will help to position your nonprofit to fundraise without the headaches of going to the bank and depositing paper checks. The online platforms will save you time and money so that you can focus on the main thing.

Secret 21 Crypto Currencies

Disclaimer:

Fundraising Secrets does not nor am I promising that you will make money or advising that you should invest into Crypto Currencies. This summary of Crypto currencies protocol is to help educate you and teach about the Crypto space. Should you need investing advice or financial advice please contact your broker, banker, CPA, accountant or any other advisors.

This summary is designed to help educate and teach you systems and processes. As always, you should do your due diligence and not invest more money than you are willing to lose in any venture or market.

Cryptocurrencies will be a new form of donations. NonProfits need to be prepared to understand this form of digital currencies. How to buy it, accept it, store it, and convert it. Cryptocurrencies is not a fad. It's actually part of a 3,000 – year old historical trend in the direction and evolution of money. Just as the internet was once said to be a fad and as we know it, the internet is here to stay and it keeps growing into mobile internet and now the "internet of things." And it's still growing.

Cryptocurrencies is here to stay. You are in the right place at the right time. James Altucher predicted that Facebook would be what it is today. He was the first to set up an online bookstore that ONLY accepted Bitcoin on Amazon. He is an expert in this space. I learned from James Altucher about cryptocurrencies and that's why I feel comfortable sharing what I've learned in this space. The cold, hard truth, if you can handle it: Up to 99% of the cryptocurrencies that exist today are total SCAMS. We'll talk about how to spot a scam in just a few moments. But first, it's important that someone in the finance department become familiar with the main points. This will position you to accept cryptocurrency donations.

What is Cryptocurrency?

A digital currency (data) in which encryption techniques are used to regulate the generation of units of currency and verify the transfer of funds, operating independently of a central bank.

What is a Blockchain?

A blockchain guarantees the correctness of its past and present data and guarantees the correctness of its future state and data.

Blockchains replace intermediaries with mathematics. Before blockchains, digital currencies had to run through central servers and be logged by central bookkeepers. Your money had to rely on several single points of failure before it would reach your intended destination.

Blockchain solved that problem.

This is all greatly oversimplifying. But it's useful. And it's a good starting point for understanding crypto.

What blockchains really mean in a nutshell:

- No geographic borders
- No banks
- Anonymity (in bitcoin, the size of the transaction can be seen, but Jon's and Joe's name can't be seen.)
- The validation is done by a computer

Buying, Selling and Securing your coins:

You can buy cryptocurrencies from a number of exchanges. Here are two that you can take a look at are:

➢ **Coinbase** - This is the one I use. I like it because it's the most established and easy to use. It's the most mainstream and has many options. Buying and selling is easy and your bitcoins are insured. Learn more about Coinbase at www.coinbase.com, you can also purchase ZRX, REP, BAT, BTC, BCH, Bitcoin, Bitcoin Cash and Ethereum (This exchange has been growing within the last several years adding more AltCoins.)

➤ **Kraken** - Another great choice. Kraken is known for its security, support and low fees. Signing up and getting started is simple. Plus there are a few more coin options to choose from. Learn more about Kraken at www.kraken.com

Both these exchanges are very easy to use. If you can use Paypal or online banking, you can figure these out fairly quickly.

How to Trade Cryptocurrencies:

You can trade crypto currencies from a number of exchanges. The one I recommend is Binance. Learn more at www.binance.com

You will create a profile and connect your bank account for deposits and withdrawals.

You must use bitcoins to trade/sell bitcoins to purchase other Altcoins.

Take a moment and listen to Episode 22 Crypto Currencies on the podcast Fundraising Secrets to fast track your understanding of Crypto Currencies.

Below is the transcription of that episode.

Cryptocurrency is a real hot topic right now and this is a great question. Should nonprofits set up an account to be able to accept cryptocurrency as a form of donation? I would probably go ahead and tell you yes, you should definitely be prepared, cryptocurrency is not going away. I've been studying cryptocurrency for about two years now and I would advise that you set up an account and just be strategic on it. I do want to give you a disclaimer however, I do not promise, or want to make any guarantees, or even advise you that you should invest in cryptocurrency, this is just a podcast to help educate you and to teach you about the crypto space. Should you need investment ideas or advice, or financial advice, please contact your broker, your bank or your CPA, your accountant or any other financial advisors in your organization. Again, this podcast is designed just to help educate you and teach you about the systems and process. As always, you should do your due diligence and not invest more money than you are willing to lose in any venture market.

So one of the things we probably want to do now is to learn crypto, so understanding what is cryptocurrency? How to buy and sell cryptocurrency, how to accept it as a donation, how to use and trade it to purchase things in your organization, how to store in a hot and cold wallet so that your cryptocurrency is safe. I would suggest that you be really diligent and do your research. Obviously Bitcoin is the Satoshi dollar that everybody is talking about and that is the one dollar that is being traded. I'll tell you exactly what the coin is a little later in this episode, but also read the white papers on every coin to spot if it's a scam or not.

A blockchain is a ledger, a ledger of how that crypto's being spent. There are also forks, there's different types of forks like the blockchain and the Litecoin and the Ethereum, they are forks of crypto, of Bitcoin and mining, how do you mine or where mining is done for cryptocurrency. So these are all some great questions and we'll dive into it just a little bit more so hold tight.

Now if you're just a moderately informed person and buying and storing crypto in the cryptocurrency space, one is you really want to get some knowledge and gain some knowledge about the space and about investment. You want to be able to go on and exchange and buy cryptocurrency, or even be able to exchange it, or secure it as a donation. You want to be able to store your cryptocurrency in a wallet and you want to back it up, you always want to use a two factor authentication on Google, two factor ... Then you can rinse and repeat that process.

So where do you want to go and get informed, or where do you want to exchange, or even maybe store your cryptocurrency? Well one space that you can get informed with, it could be

Steemit.com, S-T-E-E-M-I-T.com. YouTube is a great place, there's lots of crypto videos out there now, a lot of people have been in that space and mining and talking about cryptocurrency and trending in the market and there's a lot of podcasts on it as well. So that's some place that you can get information on your cryptocurrency.

Now there are five exchanges that I'd recommend and people really trust these and they are ones that I actually am on. I'm on Coinbase, coinbase.com. I haven't been on gemini.com, I have an account with kraken.com, abra.com is another one and then I have binance.com, Binance, I'm on Binance as well. So I'm on Coinbase, Kraken and Binance and those are where I've been storing my coins and then I take them off and put them in the wallet.

So I guess you're asking, "What is a wallet?" A storage wallet. So online, that's a wallet, but you want to also be able to store it in a hard wallet so trezor.io is a place that you can store. There's ledgerwallet.com, Ledger is the one that I go to, that's my go to, bitgo.com, that's kind of more of a Bitcoin one. Jaxx.io, J-A-X-X.io is another storage, hard wallet, MyEtherWallet.com and exodus.io. So those are a few storage wallets for your nonprofit to be able to ... but I would suggest the Ledger.

The Ledger wallet, I like it because it's a hard wallet, it's the Ledger Nano S, it looks like a jump stick drive that you'd plug into your computer and that's exactly what it is and you'd be able to back up your cryptocurrency. Now, you want to take them off of Binance or Kraken, or Coinbase, wherever you're using because what happens is, if you leave it on there, that's when it's not safe. So when they're trading and stuff, you can lose your money but if you take it and you store it, this is where you're able to have your money and not get robbed, or think that your money's been depleted into nothing, your cryptocurrency's could been depleted into nothing.

So I know I'm going through this kind of fast, and there is a lot to crypto and it should not be overlooked and you definitely should do your research and get some advice from a financial advisor or CPA, people that are in this space. Everyone is claiming to be in this space right now, but it isn't going away and the more you can get educated and the more you can get your organization organized, maybe set up an account, I would suggest Binance or even Coinbase, those two are very easy to add money to, transfer money from, Binance is one that you can transfer money from and into. You don't necessarily transfer money, you have to transfer the bitcoin itself, like XRP, or Bitcoin or Litecoin, or whatever coins you're going to be using.

The way that you can spot some fake coins is in the white papers, you have to really read the white papers to understand exactly what the function of that coin does, it has to solve a problem. If it doesn't solve a problem, then it's a fake coin. Now Blockchain is a public ledger and ... you can use Blockchain for bitcoins for each transaction and it's recorded. So in this chain, it's a ledger, Blockchain's a ledger.

Say you go to Starbucks for example and you have cryptocurrency and you want to use that. How you use it, that's a ledger. So say you have a dollar and you buying a coffee, now that ledger has been transferred over to Starbucks and now Starbucks, the next person orders coffee and they get change and they get the dollar. So all that transaction is actually in a ledger and that's how the Blockchain ledger is known, so that there's no scam. If you only have $1, you only are spending $1, so you're not going to be able to say, "Oh I have $2." No, it doesn't work like that because the ledger shows exactly and it's how the network all agrees.

So when a transaction is sent or received, the entire network, all the participants, the individuals, must agree that the currency is there in order to make the transaction occur. There are noids in place so throughout the network, they all must agree. If they don't agree then you're not able to spend that money, you don't own it.

It's funny, when I was learning about bitcoin two years ago, I was really confused on it, I still am a little confused on it, so again that's why I advise make sure you see your CPA, your bank or your financial advisor and learn from then, and know if this is an investment, but you definitely could set up your account on Binance, or Coinbase, or Kraken, or whichever one that you prefer because I feel that if ... Bitcoin is not going away, the Satoshi dollar is not going away, so you definitely want to go on Coinbase, Gemini, Kraken, Abra, or Binance. So coinbase.com, gemini.com, kraken.com, abra.com, binance.com, those are all exchanges. That's where you can exchange, sort of like the stock market but it's a different thing, but you want to set up your account there.

When you set up your account, you're not doing like dollars, the fiat, you're doing coins like Bitcoin and you can trade bitcoins. Bitcoin is not a currency, it's a technology, it's a network and a currency combined. There's over 173 countries in the world and inflation and the exchange rate varies, so that's why this was supposed to keep it a little bit more on the even keel so that people can be able to spend money if they're in the Cayman Islands, or in London, or New York, that their money is all the same because of inflation or in the exchange rate.

Again, bitcoin's not a company, it's a standard protocol operated on simple mathematical rules that everyone in the network has to agree on and how they agree on that is through the blockchains. So one more thing just before we wrap up this podcast, don't go into mining, there's just too much going on over there with mining and there's a lot of ways to spot fake coins out there, everybody thinks that they can create a coin and it's going to solve a purpose but unless you're reading the whitepaper, mining is very expensive and it also operates on your National Grid bill, or your electric bill, so you could go sky rocket high and you need space. Sometimes people, when they're doing this in their dorm or something, they're thinking that they're going to mine, the electric bill goes crazy and also the mining needs to be in a certain temperature so that it doesn't overheat and crash. So mining is really ... I don't know much about it, but I will let you know it's not something that I would advise.

Now, you can purchase using your bitcoin and your cryptocurrency, Amazon was one of the first places that you could go and do that. You can purchase a Lamborghini, there's a lot of places that you can purchase using your cryptocurrency, exchange and your vacations and things like that, buying property, real estate, you can use it at a casino, there's many places that cryptocurrency is actually coming about right now. So for a nonprofit if you are really green in this space, definitely just set up an account on binance.com and learn the language of cryptocurrency so that when people are ready to give you donations, they're able to transfer it through your Binance account.

Secret 22 Cause Marketing

Your organization probably already engages in some sort of Cause Marketing on a regular basis and should continue those ethical relationships. Cause Marketing campaigns come in all forms. Here are several different angles Cause Marketing helps your organization to earn dollars. If you're not already using these campaigns you should consider using them.

10 Types of Cause Marketing Campaigns that you'll see most often and which have proven the most effective:

1. Donation with Purchase
2. Donation with Coupon Redemption
3. Donation with Online Activation
4. The Proud Supporter
5. Buy One, Give One
6. Volunteerism Rally
7. Consumer – Directed Donation
8. Consumer Pledge Drive
9. Duel Incentive Approach
10. Request for Consumer Action

According to Cone Communications (www.coneinc.com), published article, Why Companies Want to Hire a Cause Marketing Specialist.

1. Cause Marketing Means Financial Benefits- By participating in cause marketing campaigns, companies can take advantage

of buyer enthusiasm and boost total sales. Assuming these sales are cause-driven, it's also a way for a company to bring about good works while making a profit.

2. Cause Marketing Improves Employee Recruitment, Retention, and Morale

For most people, a good chunk of their adult years will be spent at work. That's why most of us look for work environments that share or complement our values. In fact, according to the Cone Cause Evolution Study, 77% of Americans consider corporate citizenship a priority when deciding whether they want to work for a company. The same holds true for those who already have jobs:

- 72% want their employers to increase their commitment to social causes
- 88% say they feel very proud of their company's values if their company already supports a cause
- 93% expect their employers to offer opportunities to become involved with social issues Copywriting for a Cause 59 And, if a company were to shun social responsibility? Here are some other results from the same study that indicate what would happen:
- 66% would be less loyal to their jobs
- 79% would refuse to invest in company stock
- 85% of Americans said they would leave their jobs if they worked somewhere with negative social responsibility practices It's the real-life example of the Golden Rule: "Do unto others as you would have them do unto you." Except in this case, it holds true for employers, employees, and companies. A company might rephrase it to say something like, "Do unto your employees as you would have them do for your business." If you think about it, wouldn't you rather work for a company committed to your well-being and the well-being of society? Check this out: The Cone Cause Evolution and Environmental Study of MBA graduates from 11 top American and European business schools, conducted by professors at Stanford University and UC Santa Barbara, found that more than 97% of respondents were willing to give up a certain degree of financial compensation to work for a

socially-responsible company. They were open to sacrificing an average of 14% of their expected income.

This means companies can attract top talent on the merit of their culture as opposed to the salaries they offer because they're better able to:

• Attract and retain employees (the likelihood of doing this increases by 56% when a company is committed to social initiatives)
• Network with other industry leaders (54% increase)
• Keep current employees motivated (47% increase)
• Win new business contracts (27% increase)
• Maintain present contracts and customer relationships (27% increase) Each one of these business motivations translates to a more dedicated 60 Copywriting for a Cause workforce with stronger joint venture relationships. This leads to a stronger company with better profit potential.es Employee Recruitment, Retention,
and Morale

3. Cause Marketing Creates a Better Bond with Consumers- Companies have been donating money to charities for decades — long before cause marketing became popular. But they rarely made a big public announcement of the fact. It just wasn't standard practice. Target Stores, for example, has a long history of charitable giving. Initially, most of the company's philanthropic efforts were made without any form of public announcement. Then, in the 1990s, Target's competitors began announcing their own socially-responsible efforts. They were donating a lot less than Target, but they started getting nods from the public as favorable companies. The public had no idea Target had been giving back to society all along. Wisely, Target changed its strategy. The company publicly linked up with nonprofit partners and identified those partners through the sale of specific products. The result? Enormous success. Target's image was catapulted into a more favorable light. Better yet, sales increased for all the products Target sold that were linked to good causes. In the Target example, the company made it easy for consumers to see that a portion of the profits from their purchases went

to a good cause. Once Target began publicizing its corporate citizenship, consumers felt better about shopping there — a fact underscored by the spike in purchases. This is a clear example of how corporate philanthropy can shift to cause marketing when the cause efforts of a company are expressed to the public. Today, Target continues to keep up with cause marketing efforts and maintains its image as a well-respected organization. What does this tell us? Simply this: consumers have the money, and therefore the power, to make or break a company. When companies publicize the fact that a portion of their profits are pumped back into society, their reputations improve and consumer spending is almost always increased.

4. Cause Marketing Campaigns Can Increase Stakeholder Trust - We've talked a lot about how consumers play a crucial role in making a company successful. But they're not the only ones with that kind of power. The corporate world is based on investors, so keeping investors happy is another duty at the top of the list of successful businesses. When a company's corporate strategy favors responsible practices and its reputation improves, investors notice. Successful business, more or less, demands a positive reputation, so most companies will invest in things that improve their image. In turn, investors pay large sums of money to companies they believe in or which share their values. Increasingly, investors expect a company to be committed to social issues in one way or another. According to the Cone Cause Evolution Study, 66% of Americans will first consider a company's dedication to social causes when deciding where to invest their money. In fact, in the last decade, socially-responsible investments made in the United States grew 4% faster than any other sector of U.S. stocks. With numbers like that, it's obvious the majority of investors are looking for corporations with a positive commitment to society. On the flip side, consider this: When a company does not show any commitment to good causes and comes across as irresponsible to society, the Cone study shows 79% of Americans would refuse to invest in that company's stock. Plus, 74% would consider selling investments they already have in the company.

5. Cause Marketing Brings about a Substantial Image Boost- All companies are susceptible to tarnished reputations. Sometimes it's their fault and sometimes it's far beyond their control. 62 Copywriting for a Cause For example, canned-food companies may do everything required to maintain food safety standards, yet could still end up being the product behind a food poisoning outbreak and subsequent damaged reputation. Or, as was seen when Toyota recalled millions of cars for possible accelerator pedal problems, the dealerships that sold those cars ended up suffering heavy losses. Whatever the case, things happen. And when things go wrong, the media is usually quick to pounce and spread the bad news. Regardless of the origin of an image problem, the survival of a company depends on fixing the problem. Elevating and maintaining a company's image is incredibly important for survival in the business world. Cause marketing is an effective way to pull this off. Home Depot is a good example. The company has been committed to social responsibility from the get-go, but after two decades of positive business, Home Depot found itself suddenly accused of selling unsustainable products. The result was an avalanche of bad publicity. The specific problem stemmed from environmentalist groups who put together a detailed campaign announcing Home Depot's decision to sell lumber and furniture from old-growth forests. Picket lines were set up in front of the stores and the story spread like wildfire. Home Depot did two things in response. First, the company made a public commitment to phase out all old-growth wood products. They also announced public details about their partnership with home-building nonprofit Habitat for Humanity. At the time, Home Depot had already been committed to donating to Habitat for Humanity, but the company took an extra step to show the public its dedication. To start, they launched a campaign to spread the word about their commitment to building homes for those in need. Second, they donated money, goods, and employee volunteer hours to help support the campaign. What happened? Success! Home Depot's move to publicly align with a Copywriting for a Cause 63 positive cause that also complemented its business mission repaired the company's image problem and boosted profits.

Secret 23 Traffic Sources

Acquiring traffic can be tricky. The tactics behind how you get traffic on each platform are important. Because platforms such as, Google, YouTube, Instagram and Facebook, change so quickly, I've discovered a better way to help you not only get traffic but the right traffic. Let's understand the old way of getting traffic before the internet. There are 5 traffic sources.

1. Direct Mail
2. Networking
3. TV
4. Radio
5. Newspaper

The old way is still effective and used today by many nonprofits and companies. However, they won't stay ahead of the fundraising curve for long. It's time to learn new and better ways to become more efficient and stand apart from the competition. Today the new way to drive traffic a.k.a people that convert is to own your email list, be active in Facebook groups, create videos for your YouTube Channel, start a podcast, publish daily Facebook Lives and write blogs/vlogs. Being active on these platforms will help you to figure out where your ideal volunteers and donors are congregating.

This strategy of driving traffic changes the whole dynamics of how to fundraise fast for your nonprofit. These strategies of connecting people's emotions to your cause will give them the resources needed and empathy to support your mission.

Now that you have a better understanding of Sponsorship and Cause Marketing, you will want to drive traffic to your donation sites, events or volunteer opportunities. There are Three Traffic Temperature and Four Types of Traffic.

Three Traffic Temperatures

The burning love traffic: These are your raving fans. They connect with you, your company culture. They understand your mission, vision, and purpose. They donate, sponsor, and buy every product or service your organization offers.

Second, is the *MEH- Prove yourself.* These people are not raving fans as yet. The lust, luke warm kind. These people are the FREE-POO people. The type that will attend your event and travel with a zip lock bag or recycle bag and collect all the freebies your organization offers, but not make a donation or support in any capacity. We all know these people. They can be a real pain in the butt.

Third, is the *Ain't Gonna Happen:* Also known as cold traffic. Your organization has to prove itself. Although it can be very costly and hard to organize, converting them is worthwhile.

A proven way to convert this traffic temperature is to identify and qualify them. Don't change your message, change your audience, location and environment. This is what we did with the Special Olympics, NY and NAMI fashion shows. This approach resulted in 3 very profitable fundraising campaigns.

Four Types of Traffic

Traffic you Control: With Facebook moving towards charging a higher rate per click to acquire a client, it's a good idea to start building your supporters list fast using tools like ClickFunnels. Learning how to navigate other platforms such as, Instagram, Twitter, Youtube and Linkedin might just be the organic reach your organization needs to list build. Your list will become an asset that will pay your organization when hosting different campaigns. You control the budget and spend to acquire these people on which ever platform you decide to boost.

Traffic You Don't Control: It's essential to understand that no matter how much traffic you get, if you don't know how to convert that traffic, it will never help. Not knowing who you want to serve results in low conversation rate and is very costly. Traffic is the part that most people struggle with. Your organization cannot serve everyone. Hone in on your ideal avatar by demographics, age, income, zip codes, and occupation. Facebook's guidelines concerning discrimination can make list building tricky. It can be difficult to boost targeted advertisements for specific avatars such as, women, men, children, vegans, and politicians.

Traffic You Own: Here's the secret sauce. Ideal customers save you time and money. Once you own or acquire these customers you can serve them over and over again. Your cost will be minimal because you already own the list. Depending on the cost of your email management software the cost is pennies and you control this. Owning and nurturing your list is where you will want to pay the most atttention. This list becomes an asset for your organization and will pay you for a long time.

Traffic You Earn: This type of traffic is fun and most of the time costs you nothing financially. Traffic you earn is when you're invited to appear on celebrity platforms such as, podcast, TV interviews or stages to share the story of your organization. You've earned the spot light to share in the lime light of all the ethical work your organization is doing. This earned traffic source is based on of relationships and partnerships in your community and online presence. It can take months or even years to build these types of relationships. Earned traffic validation means your organization is championing the mission and getting noticed.

Chapter Four

Branding

Hosting events is one of the most profitable ways to engage your community and attract new donors by the droves. Supporters and sponsors who really believe in your organization's mission want to celebrate your organization. They want to learn more about your mission as you evolve and serve more people. Here are a few suggestions to follow when creating a signature event.

Be consistent with branding colors and images on event brochures and invitations. It's very important because you don't want to confuse the people who want to support your event.

Branding might not be the first thing you think of when you think of a nonprofit. The word "branding" sounds like something that's strictly concerning for profit businesses.

It's time that nonprofits start to think of themselves as a business and operate as such. Branding is as important for nonprofit organizations as it is for bigger for profit businesses.

If the nonprofit has been struggling to stand out amongst other similar nonprofits, it's because your message is failing to differentiate in this noisy space. Branding can help your organization become memorable. Branding can also help to build trust and loyalty. When a brand has been intentionally crafted, properly positioned and aligned to its target audience, the trust, and loyalty of the audience increases. A strong nonprofit brand creates a sense of unity and trust amongst your supporters, dream team, staff, and other stakeholders.

We can all agree that in the nonprofit sector, the competition for funding is very high. A strong nonprofit brand can help you achieve your fundraising goals by increasing visibility and generating support. Branding is more than your logo and graphics design. It's more complex process than putting your name on swag such as mugs and pens. It's a culture, plus consistency and placement. It's the organization that doesn't stop marketing on social platforms such as, Facebook Lives, LinkedIn and Instagram. The organization that markets the loudest is the category king. Your nonprofit brand is what people say about your organization when you're not in the room or on their digital device screen.

Another way to build your nonprofit brand is to start blogging on Medium.com along with podcasting on Anchor.fm. Does your organization have a podcast?

In this noisy space, I'd recommend that your nonprofit start podcasting regularly and connecting listeners to your volunteer and sponsorship opportunities. Below is a cheat sheet "How to Podcast Like a Pro!"

How To Podcast Like A Pro!

STEP 1: Pick The Best Distribution and Hosting Services For Podcast

➢ Anchor – The all in one solution for creating and distributing a podcast. (You don't own your content.)
➢ Libsyn – This is a paid hosting $5- $15 monthly. I like this hosting service the best because you do own your content.
➢ Shoutengine – awesome for just starting out
➢ Pippa.io – A new startup focusing on an easy entry into the podcasting space
➢ Simplecast – Another low – cost alternative that's worth a look
➢ Podbean- worth a look, hosting into the podcasting space

Step 2: Recording and Editing A Podcast

➢ Rev.com is my favorite to record and then transcribe for later re-purposing

➢ Audacity is my favorite FREE audio recording and editing software. –it also works on MAC and PC

➢ Garage Band is great if you have APPLE computer, or Adobe Audition if you're comfortable with Creative Cloud then ROCK On!

• Create your INTRO and OUTRO – Have A LOT of Energy when you create intro/outro.

Step 3: Which Brand Mic to buy and use for podcasting?

➢ Blue Yeti mic $149 from Amazon

➢ Phone ear piece mic (Free) not the best sound quality but works great

You can buy a mixer, but not needed. The 286s is all the mic processing you'll need if you go this route.

Step 4: Create Podcast Image

➢ Use free app Canva and design podcast image size 330 x 300

➢ Hire someone to design podcast image

➢ Get graphics and design images created for cheap on FIVERR. com

Step 5: Publish Your Podcast

➢ Record and Publish your first podcast – MY Origin Story / Back Story

➢ Follow other podcasters of influence

➢ Make a 30 list of topics by hacking what other influencers are talking about

➢ Publish at least 3 Episodes at once - Post Early, Post Often

➢ The hosting site will upload your podcast within a few minutes

➢ The hosting site will send your podcast to I-Tunes (takes up to 3-4 weeks) Stitcher app (same day) and other RSS channels for listening 2-3 days

Step 6: Be Consistent

➢ Recommend Publishing 2x-3x a week
➢ Thursday is the best day to send out new podcast episodes Post early, Post often
➢ Share your podcast on all social platforms
➢ Use older podcast episodes with newer ones to remind listeners of your story
➢ Be guest on someone else's podcast and share across channels
➢ Ask your listeners to leave 5 star reviews on Apple Podcast
➢ Have FUN!

If you do have a podcast try this easy **SCALING HACK!**

Both email methods have been tested and have been proven to gain massive results.

SAMPLE #1

Hi, {Person Name} Thank you for following me! I appreciate the love, energy and support. I'm not sure if you listen to podcasts or not, but I have a {Podcast Genre} called {Podcast Name} where I {Describe you podcast}. If you're interested, download and feel free to listen and share with me what you think. {Podcast Link}.

SAMPLE #2

Hi, {Person Name} I just wanted to express how much I appreciate the value you bring to so many people including myself. I'm a podcast host that {Describe Your Podcast} I'd be honored if you check out the show and share with me your thoughts. Also, please let me know if I can ever be of service to you. I would love to help. {Podcast Link}.

Use these samples to develop concepts and flow when reaching out to your ideal audience.

| Secret Tip #8: Start podcasting consistently.

Chapter 5

Thank Your Community

In my opinion, this is where most nonprofits fail often. They fail at thanking their community. I struggle to understand why and it frustrates me to the core. Even if I've mentioned several times how important it is to Thank Your Community in the meeting minutes, it's often ignored. The question always, replays, 'Do we have to give a plaque? Do we have to give another cheesy certificate? Do we have to send another Thank You email or letter? I get asked if the organization has to thank over again. The answer is *Yes!* When I first started to donate my time and help nonprofits to fundraise, I was having loads of fun but began slowly burning out because of the lack of appreciation. I would spend 10-12 Weeks creating and branding a 150-200 people fundraiser for free to an organization. The first year a group of us fundraised and crushed our campaign goal totaling over $600K in ten weeks. Another year, I donated 100 hours of my time and raised over $30K in 6 weeks for another organization. The third year, I tested the same blueprint and raised over $40K in ten weeks. The excitement of helping these organizations really fulfilled me. In fact, I even got my friends and family involved because it was great fun. After each event the Steering Committee would draft a survey for all who participated. We would also submit a final Recap Analysis Report to the president. I thought I did my part. I helped to raise a significant amount of money for the organization at no cost to them. I had asked the CEO for a recommendation as a token and jester of kindness and thank you. She refused. I was shocked and in disbelief. I felt I had been taken advantage of and betrayed. I'm bringing this up to point out to you the importance of Thanking Your community of volunteers and donors. Thank them more than once and often. Thank them with gifts, certificates of appreciation, and handwritten notes. Show respect and over deliver with gratitude. Be consistent and genuine. Not showing sufficient gratitude will cause people to stop volunteering with your organization. Don't let that be you. Appreciate your dream team, volunteers and community. During the event process, send a thank you to all who are actively contributing to the success of the event. You can't thank people enough for their generosity. Continue to thank your community even after the initial event. It's much easier to retain a happy and productive volunteer, than find and onboard new ones.

Two weeks after the event, host a ReCap Party to Thank volunteers and event contributors in person. Thank your Steering Committee and present them with a gift of appreciation. Have an award ceremony to present certificates of appreciation to all contributors of the event. Conclude the Recap Party with the organization's mission and announcement of the official revenues fundraised. This is very import because volunteers are driven by the impact.

| Secret Tip #9 Thank your community.

Conclusion

Nonprofits *Fundraising Secrets* offers an innovative perspective to fundraising. To survive in this competitive market your organization must begin to maximize fundraising by thinking like an entrepreneur. The government is NOT going to grant you funding easily. In fact, most nonprofits don't have systems to obtain grants. They have inadequate paper work and bookkeeping. These organizations are also lacking certain qualifications that immediately disqualify them for any grants. This is why mastering the techniques in *Fundraising Secrets* is so important. It gives you the edge to produce highly effective events, achieve your organization's goals and have a genuinely positive impact in today's world.

Fundraising Secrets teaches you step by step how to fundraise fast, grow sponsors, build a massive donor list, upsurge donations and impact the world without doing feasibility studies, needing grants, grant writers, or a large team. Just follow these proven steps and you will be successfully fundraising and building relationships globally.

About The Author

Maya McNulty is an award-winning cable lifestyle program host that has aired for over 6 years, reaching 2 million households and seen in more than 19 counties throughout New York State.

A technology maverick, Maya designed the mobile app Where to Shop and Dine, which promotes small businesses launched in 2014. She has worked with thousands of people for more than 20 years creating opportunities for entrepreneurs as one of America's most respected business branding strategist, podcaster, marketer, best –selling author and speaker. She has created spectacular events and has been recognized and received numerous awards for her career achievements and philanthropy.

Active in the community, Maya has earned the accolades of a Philanthropist. Maya has a proven record of volunteerism since she was 15 years old. Maya is the recipient of the 2018 Young Philanthropist Award from The Stakeholders Organization for her contributions to the Special Olympics, New York. She's the recipient of the 2017 Human Rights Award from The Schenectady County Human Rights Commission, 2015 Good News Award presented by the Schenectady County Chamber, 2013 Ambassador of the Year presented by Schenectady County Chamber, 2014 Path of Excellence Award presented by Time Warner Cable Business Class and 2013 Most Organized Entrepreneur Parent presented by Parentology. Maya also volunteers her time to Junior Achievement at Schenectady High School teaching Entrepreneurship to high school seniors. Maya was part of an exclusive team made up of 16 individuals making history and raising over $612,000 to fund grants and research for The Leukemia Lymphoma Society in 10 weeks.

Maya's a graduate of Bay State College, Boston, Massachusetts and Laboratory Institute of Merchandising, New York, New York with Bachelor of Professional Studies.

When not found speaking, writing or consulting, Maya finds her greatest joy spending quality time with family and friends in New York and on Sacandaga Lake.

Because of her extensive leadership and experience with entrepreneurs and nonprofits, Maya is the exemplary professional and high energy speaker for your next seminar, meeting, or company retreat.

"Maximize fundraising by thinking like an entrepreneur."

How To Order Books and AudioBooks

Book Retail - $21.99

Audiobook/CD - $37

Special Quantity Discounts

20-49 Books 10%

50-100 Books 15%

100-200 20%

200-500 30%

500+ Books 40%

*Shipping and Handling charges are additional, Please contact us for rates.

How to book Maya McNulty to maximize fundraising and inspire your next event:

Contact her at 518-441-3722

upthebiz.com

Email: maya@upthebiz.com

Fundraising Secrets Mastery

Fundraising Secrets 30 Day Challenge
www.fundraisefast.com

FUND- PRENEUR ACADEMY COURSE

Contact us for course schedule.

Website: https://upthebiz.com/

Website: https://mayamcnulty.com/

Email: Maya@UpTheBiz.com

Facebook: https://www.facebook.com/fundraisingsecrets/

Linked In: https://www.linkedin.com/in/mayamcnulty/

Instagram: https://www.instagram.com/mayamcnultyinspires/

Twitter: https://twitter.com/mayamcnulty

Download the podcast Fundraising Secrets.

Podcast: https://anchor.fm/FundraisingSecrets

Made in the USA
Middletown, DE
04 July 2019